Make Me an Instrument of Your Peace

Make Me an Instrument of Your Peace

LIVING IN THE SPIRIT OF THE PRAYER OF SAINT FRANCIS

Kent Nerburn

HarperOne
An Imprint of HarperCollinsPublishers

HarperOne

Designed by Jessica Shatan

Library of Congress Cataloging-in-Publication Data

Nerburn, Kent.
    Make me an instrument of Your peace : living in the spirit of the prayer of
Saint Francis / Kent Nerburn. — 1st ed.
    ISBN: 978–0–06–251581–0
    1. Spiritual life—Catholic Church. 2. Francis, of Assisi, Saint, 1182–1226. I. Title.
BX2350.2.N44   1999
248.4—dc21   98–43675

11 RRD(H) 15 14 13

Anything we turn in the direction of God is a prayer.

—Saint Ignatius Loyola

CONTENTS

THE PRAYER OF SAINT FRANCIS

Lord, make me an instrument of your peace.
Where there is hatred let me sow love,
Where there is injury let me sow pardon,
Where there is doubt, faith,
Where there is despair, hope,
Where there is darkness, light,
And where there is sadness, joy.

O Divine Master,
Grant that I may not seek so much to be consoled as to console,
To be understood as to understand,
To be loved as to love.

For it is in giving that we receive,
It is in forgiving that we are forgiven,
And it is in dying that we are born to eternal life.

Make Me an Instrument of Your Peace

INTRODUCTION

The Sunlight of God

When we try to understand God, we are like children trying to hold sunlight in our hands. We recognize the presence of something ineffable and mysterious, but always it eludes our grasp.

Thus it has always been, and thus it will always be. We know that, at heart, all great spiritual truths contain an utter simplicity, a shimmering depth of meaning that eludes definition and gives life a unity that no amount of analysis or knowledge can ever attain. But when we try to grasp that simplicity, we are always found wanting. We are left with the stone tablets, though we dream of being touched by the hand that gave them.

Over time we build great cathedrals of meaning and call them theology. They are brilliant monuments crafted by our intellect, worthy expressions of the best that we can do to approach the majesty and mystery of God through the mind.

But ultimately they, too, are creations of stone. They may get us closer to the ways of God on earth, but they bring us no closer to his presence.

Occasionally, in every tradition, a work emerges that seems to give us a glimpse of that presence. It seems to come from the very heart of God and to contain the mystery and majesty that we so longingly seek. It is so clear, so simple, so direct and unassailable in its spiritual truth that it transcends analysis and understanding. It is the sunlight that animates the cathedral of our theology, the touch of the hand that brings the tablets of stone.

The Prayer of Saint Francis is such a work. It shines through all the contradictions and illuminates the way of the spirit like a light from the heart of God. It asks nothing of us that we cannot do, yet it commands the impossible. It is a mighty shout from a mountaintop and a quiet entreaty whispered with bowed head. It is profoundly and decidedly Christian yet irrefutably and fundamentally universal. It is a gentle hand guiding us along the long and difficult pathway to God.

Ours is a time when people of good faith yearn for such guidance. We want to be able to walk in the way of God without closing ourselves off to the ways of others.

The Prayer of Saint Francis allows us to do so. It gives voice to our faith without asking us to turn our backs on those who have chosen other paths. It is so pure, so human, so universal in its expression, that no good-hearted person of any faith would stand against it.

There is a story told by some of the Native American peoples about the stars in the midnight sky. Each star, they say, is a hole pierced in the veil of heaven by souls that have died, and the light that shines through is the light of God, the Great Spirit, the Great Mystery.

In such a sky, Francis must be one of the brightest stars, for no one has given us more of the light of God than he. Through his life, his works, and the legacy of his joyous faith, he seems to illuminate the very center of the human heart. And nowhere does he do this more beautifully than in his gentle prayer "Lord make me an instrument of your peace."

In this beautiful and gentle prayer, he touches our deepest humanity and ignites the spark of our divinity. He makes the pathway clear, makes the stones come alive. In these few simple words, Francis places God's sunlight in our hands.

I

Lord, make me an instrument of your peace

This morning I was awakened by the trilling of a single bird. It burst like sunlight into the lambent darkness, so sweet and pure as to seem to be the first sound ever heard in all creation.

I walked to the window to listen. The bird, unaware, continued its solitary anthem. The breeze had stilled; the night rustling had subsided. Peace lay over everything. It was as if I was present at the dawn of time.

Slowly the day began to wake. Light limned the distant horizon, turning the edges of the sky to lavender. The trees began to move with the gentle breathing of the wind. All around me life was stirring. But above it all, the single voice of the solitary bird sang out in celebration of the day.

As the light grew, other sounds began. The rustle of the branches, the bark of a dog, animals scurrying, people beginning their day. And as the sounds of daily life layered across the sunrise, the bird fell silent. It had played its part. Now it gave way to other, louder voices. Its song disappeared into the music of the morning.

Such a Franciscan vision, and how close to the first line of Francis's gentle prayer, "Lord make me an instrument of your peace." It was as if the bird was offering up its own canticle to the sun, and I alone was blessed to be present to hear.

I thought of an image a teacher had once offered me. God, he said, is like a great symphony in which we must all play our individual parts. None of us can hear the whole; none of us is suited to play all the parts. We must be willing to accept the limitations of the instrument we have been given and to offer up our voice as part of the great and unimaginable creation that is the voice of God.

This bird, from the fullness of its being, was offering up its voice into that creation. I felt humbled and awed to have been in its presence.

Francis, more than any other saint, understood the godliness of music. He sang constantly. His prayers are filled with entreaties to "sing to the Lord a new song" and petitions for the earth to sing out to the Lord in praise. He was even said to stop often in the middle of a road, pick up a stick, and mimic the playing of a violin while he sang. It is as if prayer itself was song for Francis, and life itself was prayer.

Imagine what music must have been in his time. In a world with no machines, none of the background noise of modern life, and no way to capture the elusive and ethereal tones of music other than to hear them when they were created, it must have been a miraculous thing indeed to hear a sound, sonorous and haunting, created by the breath or the plucking of strings. It would rise up, like birds in flight, and float above the dross of the days, like the very voice of God itself.

What more hallowed object could have existed in such a world than something crafted by the skilled hand that could create such sounds and turn breath or touch into melody? To play an instrument would have been a divine skill. To be an instrument would have been a sacred thing indeed.

When Francis asks to be made an instrument of God's peace, he is bowing down before God's skill as maker, as musician, as composer of our days, and offering himself up to be shaped into a form through which the voice of God can be heard.

When we give ourselves to his prayer, we are asking the same.

I once had a conversation with a woman while I was on a train traveling across Canada. She was a musician—a violinist—who, as a child, had performed with major symphonies in America and Europe. She had been a prodigy, one of those rare individuals who seems to have a talent that comes from somewhere far beyond the realm of normal human affairs.

In her early twenties she had suddenly abandoned the violin in favor of the viola, the deeper-throated, less-celebrated cousin of the instrument on which she had already achieved such stunning success. It seemed an odd decision to me. She had established a promising career as a violinist; the repertoire for the solo viola is limited; and the part assigned to the viola in most musical compositions is far less significant and complex than that created for the violin.

Why, I asked her, would you turn away from an instrument of such color and vibrancy, so favored by composer and revered in the orchestra, and turn to so quiet, recessive, and generally overlooked and underappreciated an instrument as the viola?

Her answer was simple and direct.

"I like its voice," she said. "It's more me."

Like the bird singing out its solitary song in greeting of the morning, this woman was happy just to play her part, then recede as the music was taken over by the more dramatic, more flamboyant instruments in the orchestra. She knew that it was more important to play from the fullness of her being than to seek fame and favor for something that did not come from her heart.

This is the truth that Francis would have us learn.

Most of us do not live special lives. We are seldom called upon to make great pronouncements or to perform heroic deeds. We fall in love, raise children, have heartbreaks, help those in need when we can. We go to our beds at night uncertain whether our actions have had any effect.

But when Francis calls us to pray to be instruments of God's peace, he is reminding us to honor our own part in the music of creation, no matter how humble or great. He is reminding us that what we are asked to do may be no more than to offer a trill to the coming dawn or to play soft pure notes beneath the bright music of the violin. But if we humbly accept our part as a gift and play it well, we will have done our small part to help create the symphony of God's voice.

Soon enough this beautiful prayer will ask us to turn our eyes toward our responsibilities as stewards of this earth. We will be called upon to become sowers—of love, of goodness, of consolation, of hope. But for this brief moment, Francis reminds us that we are the reed through which the breath of God is blown, the strings on which the music of God is played.

For this brief moment, he reminds us, our lives are music in the heart of God.

2

Where there is hatred let me sow love

When I was eighteen and just out of high school, I worked for a summer as a groundskeeper at a country club. There was an older man who had worked there as a custodian for many years and had seen dozens of young men just like me come and go. He would watch with bemused interest as I would stumble into work on Monday mornings, haggard and bedraggled from a weekend of late hours, parties, and hard living.

He never passed judgment, never chided. But whenever he saw me looking particularly weary and disheveled, he would sidle up to me and whisper, "If you let the devil ride, pretty soon he is going to want to take the wheel and drive."

It was almost a ritual, and soon it became a running joke. But in my heart, I knew what he was saying. That simple cautionary comment probably did more to keep me on a straight path than all the lectures and sermons that I ever received.

Years later, when I worked on an Indian reservation, I saw the same lesson delivered in a different way. There was one elder in the community who had taken it upon himself to work with young people who got into trouble. The man would listen to the young person, advise them, offer them stories from their heritage, and try to teach them some of the ways of their tradition. After a period of time, if he thought he had reached the youth, he would walk over to the wall in his living room and take down a Y-shaped stick that was hanging on a hook.

One of the forking branches of the stick was painted red; the other was painted black. He would grasp the single end of the stick and hold the forked end toward the young person.

"There are two roads in life," he would say, "the red road and the black road. The red road is the way of helping and caring. The black road is the way of selfishness and hatred. The red road leads to life and light. The black road leads to death and darkness. You must choose." And he would not withdraw the stick until the young person had grasped either the red branch or the black branch.

Most of the young people grasped the red branch. "Good," he would tell them. "Now, remember this. These branches are like the red road and the black road. The further you travel along each of them, the further you are from the road you have rejected. Now go out and start walking the red road."

Like the wise janitor from my youth, this elder knew one of the great secrets of life, and it is the same secret that lies beneath the deep wisdom of the Prayer of Saint Francis. The further we travel down a certain path in life, the more that path shapes us and affects our heart and spirit.

If we set our foot upon the path of darkness, we will walk into darkness. If we set it on the road to light, we will walk toward the light. It is a fundamental law of the human heart.

When Francis tells us to sow love where there is hatred, he is invoking that same law. He is not telling us that we have to manifest love in full flower, only that we must sow a seed of love, because he knows that if we plant a seed—whether it be a seed of love, pardon, faith, hope, light, or joy—it will grow if it is tended and will soon become strong enough to stand in witness against the dark forces against which it is arrayed.

In this first invocation, "Where there is hatred let me sow love," he tests our faith in this truth to its limit.

Hatred is the most frightening of all human emotions. It is willful and predatory. It consumes everything around it. In order to keep its dark life alive, it needs an object on which to feed. If we stay near it, we know that eventually it will turn on us and try to consume us as well. It fills us with fear, and most of us, when confronted with it, simply want to get away.

But Francis tells us to stay present to it. Meet hatred with love, he tells us. If we run from it, we are only letting the world move further down the black road. We must have faith that the seeds we can plant in another's heart will blossom into something good.

But how are we to do this? Our love is fragile, compromised, riddled with self-interest. Hate seems so pure and active and strong. Perhaps the great spirits among us—the Gandhis, the Mother Teresas, the Francises and Martin Luther Kings—have the strength to sow love in the face of hatred. But most of us are too small; our hearts are too ordinary. When we are confronted by hate, we want to run away, lest it do violence to our body or spirit or those we love.

But Francis understands the human heart better than we. He knows that love is stronger than hate because hate is an active, predatory force proceeding from an empty center. It lashes out at everything around it, but at its core is a loneliness or a deep hurt or sadness that has become so calcified that the only way it can be expressed is in a desire to destroy all things good and gentle and kind. A love, even the most fragile love, can conquer hate, because the empty center at the core of hate is always silently crying out to be filled with love.

If we think about the meanest, most hate-filled people we know, chances are we have seen a tiny place where they, too, can be touched—thoughts of a grandchild, the love of a dog or kitten, a memory of better times. But they are so armored in their hatred that they don't want us to see this. They will go to any length to hide their softness, because it is a window into the vulnerability of their own hearts, and the only protection they have is in the armor of their own hate.

But if we take the chance and plant a seed of love—knowing that the ground on which it falls, though rocky, still has enough goodness for love to take root and grow—a miracle can occur.

Each year I rediscover this truth during the Christmas season, when I take my red velvet Santa suit from the closet, daub my nose and cheeks with rosy makeup, attach a long, wavy, white wig and beard, and go out into the streets to offer the presence of Santa to whomever I might meet.

I never know what is going to happen. I have found myself in nursing homes where men and women lifted themselves from their wheelchairs to sit in my lap. Fights in bars have stopped simply because I have walked through the door. I have had retarded people burst into song when they saw me pass. I have had a mother stop me on the street and lead me to her home so I could sit and hear the Christmas wishes of her sick child.

White, Black, Chinese, Indian, young, old, Christian, Jew—it does not matter. When I am Santa there are no barriers of race or age or wealth or faith. For Santa is the innocent dream of childhood, and when I am Santa I am trusted and embraced by every person who still keeps that dream alive in their heart.

I remember one instance when I put on my Santa suit and drove to a particularly violent part of town. It was a housing project notorious for gangs and drugs, and the residents lived in fear behind locked doors and barred windows.

I had stepped from my car and started to walk toward a community center a block away. I always tried to park a distance from my destination, because it seemed wrong for children to see Santa stepping from the driver's seat of a car. As I was walking, a group of teenaged boys gathered around and began taunting me. This was not joking; it was blood sport. Something bad was going to happen.

Soon another group of young men in their early twenties came cruising up in their car. There were about six of them. They, too, were obviously up to no good. When they saw what was taking place they hopped out and came toward me. I expected the worst and had images of being left beaten and bloody on the sidewalk of one of the meanest streets in town.

But the young men walked right past me to the teenagers. The biggest and most threatening of the men grabbed one of the younger boys by the scruff of his neck and said, "You don't mess with Santa." Then, turning to me, he said, "Sorry, Santa. These kids are just ignorant. Come on. You got work to do."

He led me through the neighborhood, building by building, to places where, under normal circumstances, I never would have dared to go. I can still remember the sound of the unlocking doors every time someone looked out from behind barred windows and saw that it was Santa at their step.

Soon people were coming out into the street and children were flocking around me. The young boys who only minutes before had been my harassers now were organizing the children into lines, telling them to behave and to wait nicely for their chance to talk with Santa.

There is not a person living on that street who would not tell you that it is a dangerous place, filled with drugs and crime and hate. But on that day, doors were opened, and we all had a glimpse into the unprotected human heart. And what we saw was not hate, but the deep and unquenchable desire to give and receive love.

It is moments like this that must give us the courage to sow love in the face of hate. For if we don't—if we turn away or meet that hate with a hatred of our own—we are allowing the darkness in the world to increase. We are refusing to trust in the power of our own love, and by turning away, we are allowing the world around us to travel a little further down the road to darkness.

There is a story told about one of Francis's followers, a Brother Angelo, who one day heard a knock on the friary door at Monte Casale. When he opened the door, he saw three beggars whom he recognized as three dangerous criminals who had been on a rampage of murder and robbery throughout the region.

The presence of the men upset him greatly. He started yelling at them, "It's not enough that you rob honest folk of the fruit of their toil. Now you want to take the little belonging to God's servants!"

Then he turned them away, shouting after them, "You are unworthy of a place on earth. You have no respect for men and hold God who made you in contempt. Get out of here, and don't let me see you again!"

When Francis returned from a day of begging, he was informed of what Brother Angelo had done. Immediately he demanded that Brother Angelo take wine and bread to the men and apologize to them for the way he had treated them. He pointed out that Jesus had instructed his followers to minister to the sick, not to the healthy. With that he sent the monk forth to find the robbers and murderers he had turned away.

In the story, the criminals, of course, repent their sins and embark upon a life of penitence and contrition. In the world in which we live, this does not always happen. In fact, the sad truth is that it seems to happen infrequently, if at all.

But the point is well taken. If we concern ourselves only with the good people on earth, we are not truly doing God's work. And if we allow the hateful actions of others to determine our response to them, we are becoming mirrors to their hate. We are allowing them to set our foot upon the black

Kent Nerburn

road that they are already traveling and moving us all further from the path of love that we know is the way of God and the way of life.

It is easy to turn away from hatred and hide behind a cloak of righteousness, as Brother Angelo did. It is even easier to focus only on the goodness in life and ignore the hatred that does not touch us directly. But Francis, who saw beauty and brightness everywhere, challenges us from the very outset of his prayer to stare hatred in the eye and trust in the power of our own love to stand against it.

This is no small challenge. It asks us to overcome our fear and to have faith in the power of goodness. It asks us to believe that our own halting love is strong enough to take root in a field that seems choked with the weeds of hate.

But Francis would not have placed this entreaty first if he did not think it was all-important. He wants us to stand up for our belief that we can make a difference. He wants us to realize that even in the presence of something as frightening and predatory as hate, our own small love, struggling and fragile as it is, can prevail.

Remember, he reminds us, that love is a habit of the heart, an inclination of the spirit. Each day, a thousand times and in a thousand ways, we are all called upon to make choices that incline us toward the darkness or toward the light. They are not all significant choices; some of them may hardly seem like choices at all. But each of them moves our heart a little further along the red road or the black.

If we can get someone who is filled with hate to make just the smallest of choices in favor of goodness and love, we are moving their heart further from the path of darkness and further along the path of light.

We have sowed the seed of love in that empty place at the center of their heart, and though they may not notice, love has taken root and begun to come alive.

What they don't realize, and what Francis reminds us, is that this small flowering of love, seemingly so insignificant and inconsequential, will continue to grow. It will become part of the legacy that they carry with them as they travel through life.

And if we can get them to bring this bit of love and goodness along on their journey, something strange and miraculous may just happen. Pretty soon that love may not be satisfied just to be along for the ride. Pretty soon it may want to take the wheel and drive.

3

Where there is injury let me sow pardon

I once spoke with a man who had done hard time at a maximum security penitentiary. I asked him what had been the single most significant lesson he had learned from being inside. He looked at me with sad eyes and said, "You would not believe what lives inside the human heart. There really is such a thing as evil."

I have never quite gotten over the chill that his words sent through me. And as much as I would like to believe otherwise, the occurrences that take place in the world on a daily basis make his assertion almost impossible to deny.

What, then, are we to make of Francis's command to give pardon where there is injury?

Are we to believe that we are to forgive all manner of crimes and transgressions, no matter how monstrous?

Are we called to achieve some elevated state of spiritual enlightenment wherein we accept the evils of the world as somehow reflecting some higher divine purpose?

Or is this command of Francis's merely the blithe platitude of a man who lived unencumbered on the earth and never had to face such questions as what to do if a madman breaks into your home and murders your family?

These are questions that beset the earnest seeker who would try to walk Francis's path through a world of dark realities. And they admit of no easy answers. But I once had an experience that gave me insight into what some of those answers might be.

I was present in a courtroom where a young man was on trial for murdering a girl he had seen walking down the street. He had not known her personally. She had wronged him in no fashion whatsoever. Her crime was simply being young and alive and in the wrong place at the wrong time. He and a friend had dragged her into the woods, placed a gun behind her ear, and blown off the back of her head.

The prosecuting attorney described in grim detail the specifics of the murder and held up a bloody paper bag that contained the clothes of the young victim. The horror was almost too much to bear. Most in the courtroom averted their eyes. But through it all the father of the murdered girl sat impassively, watching the trial, watching the boy.

After the trial was over, and the boy was found guilty, the father announced that he was going to visit that boy in jail and get to know him.

People were appalled. Why would anyone who had suffered what this man was suffering undertake such a task?

But the father was adamant. "That boy and I are forever bound," he said. "We need to know each other. I do not know if I can forgive him. But perhaps if I know him I will not hate him. This is about healing and reconciliation."

In that moment, the insight of Francis became clear to me. When he tells us to sow pardon, he is telling us to seek healing and reconciliation, not approval or even acceptance. There was no way that the father of the murdered girl was ever going to give approval to the boy for what he had done. It is not even clear that he could ever find it in his heart to accept the unthinkable event that had occurred, though clearly he was trying to do so. But he could seek to reconcile two men whose lives were forever linked through the person of a young woman and to bring forth some measure of understanding and, hopefully, creative growth in the aftermath of a horrible event.

This is a hard issue. Most of us would not have the power to make such an effort. I know that I do not have that greatness of spirit. But I also know, in my heart of hearts, that the grieving father was making the correct choice. He was trying to move the world forward from a point of horror and to turn a circumstance so dark that few can imagine it into a moment of healing and growth.

The key is in the word *injury*. Francis did not say, "where there is wrongdoing, let me give pardon," or "where there have been crimes, let me offer pardon." He said, "where there is injury, let me sow pardon." And injury implies the possibility of healing.

Healing rises above the question of right and wrong, even good and evil. It has to do with restoring a life to health.

If we are able to look upon pardon not just as forgiveness, but as doing what is necessary to restore health to the body or spirit, Francis's injunction suddenly seems less impossible and disconnected from our lives. In fact, it seems like the wisest of counsel.

The father of the murdered girl cannot change what has occurred. He may forever wonder why such an event had to take place and wrestle with a dark angel in his heart until the day he dies. But he cannot change the fact that the event happened.

What Francis is telling us is that when such incomprehensible events occur, our goal should be to promote healing in any manner of which we are capable. It is the only way that we can free ourselves from a frozen scream in time and fulfill our responsibilities as co-creators of meaning in this universe.

Once again, we must remember that Francis calls us only

to "sow." "Sowing" does not imply that something is fully grown, only that the seeds of possibility have been planted. Even if the father of the murdered girl cannot find the slightest possibility of forgiveness in his heart, by seeking reconciliation and healing on some level, he is sowing the seeds of the possibility of pardon and forgiveness at some future time.

Perhaps this will happen. Perhaps it will not. It is not up to him to say whether the seeds he plants will fall on fertile ground. That is where faith in the goodness and mercy of God comes in. But even if he spends the remainder of his days gnashing his teeth, rending his garments, and shaking his fists at the heavens, he is leaning in the direction of hope. He is saying that even though he doesn't understand, and can't understand, he is trying to heal. And in the intention lives the seed of a possible resolution.

There is a famous passage in the book of Exodus where Moses and Aaron ask the pharaoh to let their people leave Egypt. Over and over the pharaoh refuses. And each time, we are told, the pharaoh's heart was hardened.

This same hardening of the heart occurs in each of us when we do not lean in the direction of healing. With each passing day, and each refusal to seek reconciliation, we become more callous and closed to the possibility of reconciliation. And the wound caused by the injury becomes more and more a part of our being.

If we seek healing, it is true that the wound may still become an awful scar. But at least life goes forward. When an injury is not allowed to heal, the wounded person dies.

This is what happens to us when we refuse to sow healing and reconciliation. Our hearts and spirits die. Perhaps this is what we want. Perhaps this is our monument and testament to what we have lost. But it is not the course that Francis would have us take. He would have us sow the seeds of pardon, no matter how difficult that sowing might be.

Luckily, most of us, in our daily lives, are not confronted with such mortal injuries as the father who lost his daughter. The injuries we create, and the injuries we experience, are usually but small slights and affronts. The labors required to begin the process of healing are not great. It is a constant measure of our humanity to rise above these injuries and to forgive those who cause them even as we forgive ourselves when we cause injury to others.

I often think of the way the Dakotah Indians responded to a small wrong. When, for example, a young person walked between an elder and a fire—an act of profound impoliteness in their culture—the young person said, simply, "Mistake." It was an honest acknowledgment of an error of judgment, devoid of any self-recrimination or self-diminution. All present nodded in assent, and life went on.

How healthy such an attitude seems. We all commit mistakes in judgment, and we all need forgiveness. If we had the option of making a simple acknowledgment of our mistake and then going on with our affairs, how much clearer and gentler life would be. And how much healthier would our own hearts be if we looked upon the injuries caused us by others as simply the mistakes of human beings who, like us, are struggling to get by in a complex and mysterious world.

Our lives brush clumsily against the lives of others. A wrong word, a rash action—these are as much a part of our lives as the caring gesture and the loving touch. We are all guilty of them; we all receive them. There is no surprise when they come, issuing forth either from us against others or from others against us. The only surprise is that we never cease to make such errors and that we have such difficulty forgiving them when they are committed against us by others.

It is our daily task in life to find a way to forgive these errors, in ourselves and in others, without ignoring or diminishing the wrong that has been done. And if the crime is so great that we cannot find it in our heart to offer forgiveness, at least we can make the first steps toward healing. Perhaps, with time and the grace of God, forgiveness, too, will result.

What Francis is calling us to do is to live a life that stands for healing, however we are able to offer it. Yes, we may confront evil in this world. Yes, we may experience wrongs that defy our capacity for forgiveness. But if, like the distraught father of the murdered girl, we take the first tentative steps toward healing, we are sowing the seeds of pardon. And where the seed of pardon is planted, the flower of true forgiveness may someday bloom.

4

Where there is doubt, faith

The other day a young man came to my door. He was earnest, bright, and on a mission.

Did I know Jesus as my personal savior? Did I know that God had a wonderful plan for my life?

He obviously had not been at this long. He was nervous and uncertain. His clothes were too new and a bit ill fitting. He looked for all the world like a young salesman out on the street for his first cold call. And in many ways he was. But what he was selling was his vision of God's truth, and this buoyed him up. As I listened and did not reject him, he gained courage and confidence.

Would I like to sit and talk about Jesus? Did I ever have doubts about my own life? Would I like to read the Bible with him?

I liked him. In some ways, I envied him. He was on fire with his faith. And though he was obviously fulfilling some obligation to his church by knocking on doors, he was doing it with a joyful spirit.

His presence, more than his words, challenged me. Is this what my faith should be? By failing to profess publicly, am I keeping my light under a bushel and acting as one of those of whom Jesus spoke when he said, "If you are lukewarm I will spit you out of my mouth"?

I do not want to be lukewarm. I do not want to be spit out of God's mouth. I want my faith to offer light and consolation to others. But I cannot, in good conscience, force my faith on others. I have seen too much of the world to believe in the primacy of my own belief. I would rather try to manifest my belief in God than to profess it.

Yet the words of Francis haunted me. Would he not be out on the streets professing his faith, seeking to share it, challenging those who are silent to cast off the shackles of their uncertainty and sing out the joyful song of the Lord?

Perhaps. But we live in a complex time. We have seen too much of the warfare wrought by faith turned into ideology, too much of the true believer turned zealot. We know that other people of good heart and a deep faith in God have, at other times and places, chosen spiritual paths very different from our own. It seems an affront to the richness of human experience and, indeed, to the very omnipotence of God to assume that the truth we have been given is the only truth there is.

Are we truly so bold as to say that our way is the only way? There are many among us, like the young man at my door, who believe that we must. They see any way other than their own as a path of darkness, and they believe in their heart of hearts that they must suffer any personal indignity and go to any length to get people to believe as they do. Their God, they believe, demands it.

But I cannot share their conviction. I have watched the pious Jew walking his son to temple; I have heard the Native American woman softly telling her children to learn the ways of love from the animals in the woods. I have seen the deep peace and serenity of the Buddhist who humbly rises from quiet meditation.

To me, God wears many masks and speaks in many voices. I cannot, in good heart, believe that these people are not walking a path to God that is as worthy, as true, as the one that I, or the young man at my door, have been given.

How, then, am I to meet Francis's injunction to sow faith where there is doubt when I myself will not claim the universality of my own faith and would rather genuflect to God in private than to sing his praises in joyful public celebration?

The answer, I believe, can be found in Francis's own words—to sow faith where there is doubt. For even if we do not believe in our right to shape the faith of others, that does not mean we cannot try to sow seeds of faith that they can shape themselves. It is to their doubt that we are called to minister, not to their faith. And this is a ministering that all of us who share a belief in God—however we understand that God—can perform.

Doubt is a part of the human condition. We doubt our ability to be good parents, to be good children, to meet all the obligations that confront us in the course of a day. Yet that does not immobilize us. We go forward with such faith as we have, making progress by halting steps, striving ever toward the light. Yet we do not see this as faith, only as the necessary labor of a life well lived.

But when it comes to faith in God, we have no confidence in the worthiness of our own struggle. We believe faith should come across us like a blinding light, transforming us, subsuming us in divine rapture. We want to be like Paul on the road to Damascus, knocked to the ground by a truth we cannot deny. If our faith is not like this, we reason, it is no faith at all.

But faith is not always so dramatic. It is sometimes a quiet shaping—an edifice built, stone by stone, from the hard labors of our heart.

I once spent time in a Benedictine monastery creating a sculpture for the abbey. The monks were good and holy men,

Kent Nerburn

but I found myself growing increasingly unhappy with what I perceived to be their harshness of heart and lack of empathy and compassion for the suffering in the world around them.

The abbot, seeing this in me, took me aside. "Stay in the machine," he said. "It will clean you out." It was a strange comment and quite out of keeping with his normal way of speaking. But in the months that followed, I came to understand what he meant. I devoted myself to the Benedictine spiritual path and soon came to see, if only dimly, the great spiritual light toward which it pointed.

Far from lacking compassion and empathy for the poor and suffering, these men had made a conscious decision to disengage themselves from the ephemeral concerns of the world so they could devote themselves ceaselessly and with absolute spiritual focus to the task of praying for the souls of all people, rich and poor, living and dead. "Let others minister to the needs of the body," they reasoned. "It is our spiritual mission to focus on the needs of the soul." In their own fashion, and with great purity of spirit, they were playing their part in the great symphony of God. I simply had not been attuned to the unique voice of Benedictine spirituality.

Eventually the sculpture was finished, and I left the abbey. The Benedictine way was not my way. But, like a sailor passing the shoreline of a beautiful and unimaginable country not his own, I had glimpsed a truth so great and transforming that it was beyond imagining.

Had I stayed in the monastery, I do not believe that I ever would have had a transformative experience of the sort that I associate with conversion. But day by day, year by year, I would have had my spirit infused with a glow that eventually would have taken over and transformed my entire being.

This is what the abbot had been counseling—spiritual formation, not spiritual conversion, the gradual opening of the heart, through diligent and humble work, to an awareness of a deeper spiritual truth.

This is the path most of us must walk to faith. It is the same type of spiritual endeavor undertaken by the devout Hindu who submits to the long and rigorous journey toward spiritual clarity through the practice of yoga. It is the same type of spiritual labor undertaken by the Lakotah youth who goes forth year after year in search of a vision, or the Dakotah mother who sets a child beneath a tree to listen to the music of the branches and to learn from the activities of the birds. Though the vision of God each attains may be different, their method of spiritual development is the same. They set their feet upon the path, incline their hearts toward the light, and trust in the truth toward which they journey.

At first, any of these enterprises may seem wholly without purpose. But we must suspend disbelief in order to move toward belief. If we do not, we give up, leave, and dismiss the exercise as one of futility and delusion.

But if we persist—if we have faith—gradually, slowly, and with a growing sense of intensity and inner ratification, the activities we perform begin to shape our consciousness and to inform and color our spirit. The skepticism and doubt with which we began are gradually suffused with light, and faith begins to live where once only doubt was able to reside.

This is how we can sow faith where there is doubt, even if our own faith is not an incandescent flame. We take such spiritual gifts as we have and use them to set others on their own spiritual paths, whatever those paths might be.

We each have seeds that we have been given to sow. They are the gifts of our own spiritual insight. Do we have a steadfastness of purpose? A sense of prayerful watchfulness? Do we have a deep sense of compassion for other human beings or a deep apprehension of the reality of God? Perhaps we have a love of Jesus or a deep awareness of the dharma. Or a knowledge of the music sung by the winds in the trees.

These gifts may not be blinding, overwhelming testimonies of personal faith, but they are a starting point on a spiritual journey.

I often think of the poignant story in the Gospels about the woman who had been hemorrhaging for twelve years.

She had gathered in a crowd that was pressing upon Jesus as he spoke.

"If only I can touch his cloak," she thought, "I shall be healed."

Quietly, she made her way forward and touched the hem of Jesus' cloak. Immediately, she was made well.

It was the merest touch of the cloak that healed her. She was not raised up, singled out, and embraced. She was not subsumed into some great light of truth. She humbly came forth, brushed against God where she could, and had faith that she would be made whole.

Sometimes we must be satisfied just to touch the cloak of God—to brush against great spiritual truths with our own spiritual gifts, however humble they may be.

We must never lose sight of the fact that faith is not the same as certainty. If it were, it would be knowledge. Faith is the great leap across the chasm of the unknown into the uncertain darkness. It is the capacity to step with confidence where there is no knowledge, to move forward in the darkness toward the light, however small that light may be. Did not even Jesus, in his moment of darkest fear, cry out, "My God, my God, why have you forsaken me?" Should we, then, be so unaccepting of our own doubt and so critical of it in others?

We must remember that more people live in the shadow of doubt than in any blinding light of faith. When we show others that we, too, struggle with doubt but continue to walk forward in faith toward that distant and unfathomable light, we meet them in the shadow of their uncertainty and bear witness to the worthiness of their struggle. We strengthen their courage to reach out for the cloak of God in their own way. And in doing this, we sow seeds of faith as surely as if we were on fire with a private belief, professing with certainty and conviction.

We must witness what we can and point that witness toward the light of God. Feed the hungry, comfort the lonely, visit the sick, assist the fallen—whatever it is that we can do to increase the light of goodness, that is where our witness begins.

Speak of our God, manifest our faith, allow others to see that even though we do not feel we have a claim on absolute truth, we have a peace in our heart that comes from believing that there is an eternal truth from which we come and to which we shall return. Let others know that our faith honors their faith and meets it with a humble sense of respect and recognition.

As I stood on my doorstep, looking at the young boy before me, at once so fragile and so on fire with his faith, I knew that the measure of my faith was not that it should be as incandescent as his but that I should be able to embrace him in his own fledgling witness.

Perhaps, then, when he meets someone equally alive with a faith other than his own, he will remember the man who embraced his witness and, rather than contending, will embrace the witness of this person who knows their God by a different face or a different name.

This, I must believe, is what Francis would have me do. In this world, where skepticism and disbelief are seen as badges of intellect and conflicting faiths clash like armies in the night, my willingness to embrace varieties of belief and to stand humble before them all is as worthy a sowing as any profession of a blinding personal faith.

Though Francis himself, on fire with a blinding faith, might under the same circumstances be dancing and singing out to his God, there are many rooms in our Father's mansion. Surely he would not disdain those of us who choose a more quiet witness and humbly seek to lead those of weaker heart toward that mansion, no matter through which door it is they choose to enter.

5

Where there is despair, hope

Despair is perhaps the greatest of crimes against the human spirit. It cries out that our world is not great enough to overcome the darkness that surrounds our heart. It rips from God and the universe the possibility of redemption. It robs us of hope.

Who knows the moment when deep sadness turns to despair and the flickering light of possibility is snuffed out, leaving us to sit numbly before the dark march of meaningless time?

When despair comes across a person, there is no logic, no word of consolation, that can offer meaningful balm. The despairing soul sits empty eyed, neither seeing nor caring. And all words of consolation clatter like dry bones upon the floor.

How, then, are we to give hope where there is despair?

I remember years ago when I was living in a small town in Germany. I was surrounded by an unutterable and inconsolable loneliness. I knew no one. I did not have my language. And each day I dropped deeper into a sadness that seemed to have no bottom.

One day, seeking to escape myself, I took a train to a distant town where an American movie was showing. I hoped that hearing my own tongue and seeing images of my own homeland would lighten my spirit.

I arrived several hours before the film was to begin. So I sat on a bench on a street corner and watched the town shut down for the evening. One by one the shopkeepers shuttered their windows, locked their doors, and hurried to the buses and cars that would take them to homes and family. No one gave me so much as a glance as they passed.

Darkness moved across the hills. Lights went on in distant houses. Soon the town was empty, and I was alone with only the dark shapes of my imagination to keep me company.

In the distance, far up the street, I heard a strange, muffled sound. I looked up and saw a man coming toward me. He was wearing a suit, but his shirt was out and his tie was askew. His gait was unsteady; he lurched and fell against the buildings as he walked. He was obviously drunk. And he was sobbing.

In my months in Germany, drunks had become my friends. They, too, were often lonely. They did not care about my halting language, and in a country where I had made so few connections, they often opened up to me with the fullness of their hearts.

I smiled as the man stumbled toward me.

"Guten Abend," I said.

He stared back at me with the saddest eyes I had ever seen. Tears rolled down his cheeks. I do not believe that I have ever seen, before or since, such a tortured look upon the face of another human being.

He began sobbing again and buried his face in his hands. His body racked and heaved. He seemed about to come apart.

"Sitzen Sie," I said.

"Danke," he responded, and almost fell to the ground beside me. There, in the gloaming, we sat, struggling to find a common language with which to communicate. My German was poor but workable. His English was good but long forgotten. In a clumsy mix of our own two tongues, his story came out.

He was a judge, well respected in the community. That morning, a young girl had run in front of his car as he was driving to work. There had been no time to stop. He had struck her, killing her instantly. He had been wandering the streets, drinking, ever since.

"I am a judge," he kept saying. "I am a judge. How could I have done this?" It was as if his station in life and claims on respectability should have protected him against so horrible an event. And even more, he felt he had betrayed the trust of the entire community.

With my fumbling German, I tried to find words that would calm his spirit. But there was no consolation I could offer. He knew that it was not his fault; he knew that it had been an accident. "I keep seeing her in front of me," he sobbed. "Why could I not stop?"

I tried again to speak some words that would matter, but he stopped me. "Don't talk," he said. "I don't need words. I just need to be near somebody."

I stayed with him on that street corner long into the night. He did not wish to go anywhere. He did not wish to talk. Occasionally he would take my hand; occasionally he would be overcome with deep and heaving sobs. But whenever I tried to leave or allow him the privacy of his own grief, he would say "No" and grab my hand to make me stay.

That night I learned something deep about despair and what it means to offer hope. It is the gift of our presence that the despairing soul needs, no more, no less.

When we sit with someone in despair, we are sitting in vigil. We cannot reach their consciousness with ours, nor can we offer consolation that will touch their darkness. Like Jesus in the Garden of Gethsemane, they want only that we should sit and watch with them.

Despair is a sickness of the soul. If the despairing soul is to heal, it will do so on its own. The greatest gift we have to offer is our selfless and solitary witness. For when we stand vigil with the despairing spirit, more than anything else we are denying the emptiness into which the spirit wishes to plunge. By our presence we are affirming a worth that the spirit does not feel. We are bearing witness to a possibility in which the spirit does not believe. We are defying the darkness.

To help another stand against despair, as I tried to do that night, it does not matter what our station or status in life might be or even if we believe ourself to be a good and caring human being. The hope we offer is the simple presence of another spirit, less overwhelmed with darkness, that refuses to withdraw its light.

This may not seem like hope. It may not seem like anything at all. But against true despair, only a strong and courageous spirit can stand. After all, even the disciples abandoned Jesus at his greatest moment of darkness and doubt.

If we are able to stay with someone at their time of darkness and doubt and simply bear witness, we are performing a holy act, and the wounded heart will know. By the mute testimony of our presence, we are saying, "You are a child of God, and you matter." And that is sometimes enough to make a wounded heart turn back, if only for a moment, and feel the presence of the light.

6

Where there is darkness, light

For all the beauty of this wonderful prayer, there is about it an optimism and gentleness that sometimes seem to exclude those of us who are experiencing moments of deep darkness in our lives.

"Where there is hatred, let me sow love." "Where there is sadness, let me sow joy." These are fine sentiments for those of us who feel that we have within us something to give. But where are we to turn when we ourselves are broken—when we feel no love, when we contain no joy, when we are empty husks with no seeds to sow, no life to give? Are we then thrust back upon the darker prayers—the Twenty-third Psalm with its comforting words to those who must "walk through the valley of the shadow of death," or Jesus' desperate cry in the

Garden of Gethsemane—as we search for consolation? Does Saint Francis's gentle prayer have nothing to say to us in moments such as these?

I used to feel that this was true. I would turn away from the prayer in moments of sadness or personal desolation. Saint Francis was, I reasoned, one of God's blithe spirits, a celebrant of life, and his prayer was meant as gentle guidance for those moving toward the light. To those of us whose lives had descended into darkness or tragedy, the prayer had no relevance. When the cup passed from us, if indeed it did, we could turn again to Francis and his hopeful words and resume our task of seeking to be an instrument of God's peace. But for the moment of darkness, the words of Francis did not seem to offer consolation to the soul.

But as I have lived with this prayer I have come to think otherwise. I have found that it contains a special wisdom for times of deep personal travail. And true to Francis's spirit, it is wisdom not so much of consolation, but of hope.

This wisdom first came home to me one morning twenty years ago on a desolate beach in Mexico. Nursing a deep wound from a lost love and confused about the direction of my life, I had journeyed to this lonely and forsaken outpost to reassess my dreams and contemplate the bleak prospects of my own inner horizons.

The beach was a long crescent that jutted out into an azure

Kent Nerburn

sea. A small village stood huddled on its shore. This was not the kind of village in the travel brochures, with whitewashed buildings and colorful markets. It was a rude and brutal collection of shacks and lean-tos set around a small dusty square in an isolated part of the country, far from amenities and any sense of civilization as I knew it. Families lived in hovels made from abandoned car hoods and pieces of cardboard; there were no schools for a hundred miles; and in the evening the young men drank beer and tied dogs to the bumper of an old pickup truck and dragged them around the town square until they died.

There were few tourists—only an occasional sport fisherman or naturalist who had come to study the abundant marine life that lived off this particular coast. I had chosen the spot at random on a map and driven there almost as an act of defiance, covering the last fifty miles across the desert mostly by dead reckoning, as the road was little more than a vague imprint of ruts in the hard sand and sagebrush.

On this particular morning, while walking around the edge of the bay, I saw an object floating in the water. At first I thought it was a large fish washed up or some variety of sea turtle. But on closer examination, it proved to be the body of a man. He was wearing American clothes.

I took the identification from his pocket and ran back to the town to inform whatever authorities I could find. I was directed to a small trailer, where a local official informed me that I would have to remain in the town until the matter was sorted out.

I wandered around in the unforgiving heat, trying to occupy my time. I soon noticed a woman, an American, walking frantically along the beach. She was looking for her father, who had been raised in this village and now had come back for a visit. He had gone off the night before to play cards with some other men, and she had not seen him since.

I sat her down and told her what had just occurred and the name that had been on the identification. She let out an inconsolable wail and buried her face in her hands.

I put my arm over her shoulder and sat silently with her as her body convulsed with sobs. Far out across the bay I could see the dark lump in the water and the lonely sentinel who had been sent to stand guard until more significant authorities could arrive from Ensenada, several hundred miles away.

It was a horrible scene, a surreal scene, one that is etched for all time in my memory. But it is also a scene that taught me a great lesson. For though I felt empty and depleted with nothing to give to anyone, all my life experience—my years of assisting my father as he counseled disaster victims and their families, my seminary training in meeting people at the point of their spiritual need, my comfort in isolated settings, even the deep darkness of the spiritual desolation that was engulfing me at that time, and the simple fact that I was an

American—made me the right person at that moment to offer such small comfort and assistance as this poor distraught woman and her family needed.

For the next day I spent every moment at their sides, standing in silent witness while they mourned or doing whatever was required to help them survive the ordeal that had been visited upon their lives. I did not eat; I did not sleep. I did not think of myself or my situation. I did not watch, with a third eye, the actions that I was performing. For that brief moment, I was outside of myself, living only in the present, giving what was needed from unknown reservoirs of my own being, with no thought or awareness of the significance of my actions or consideration of any good that I might be doing.

Eventually the authorities released the body, and I accompanied the grieving family in a macabre cortege led by an ancient Mexican hearse that slowly wound its way across the barren mountains and arroyos to the town of Ensenada. There, a local mortuary arranged to have the body of the father sent back to his home in the States.

When the ordeal was finally under control—when all the officials had been paid, all the papers had been signed, and we had all made our way safely back to the American side of the border—the woman came and hugged me as if I were her last link to life itself. "Thank you for helping to lead us home," she said softly. Then she drove away.

I have never seen that woman since. I do not know her name. I do not know when or how or where her father was buried. I only know that for one brief moment I was called upon to bring light into a great darkness, and I did so. For that brief moment the darkness of my own heart meant nothing. I was truly an instrument of God's peace, and for that I shall always feel humbled and blessed.

That time in Mexico has always stayed with me, not only because of the stark and horrific tableau that it presented, but also because of the unexpected strength of spirit that I was able to find in myself at a moment when I was convinced that there was no light in me to give to anybody. But, in truth, I did have light, though I myself was aware only of my own darkness. And the small light that I had proved to be a great light in the life of another.

This is the consolation that Francis's prayer has to offer those of us engulfed in our own darkness. It does not call us to *be* light, only to *give* light. We are not the way, the truth, and the light, and we are not asked to be. We are but a brief candle that must not be kept under a bushel. Our task is simply to offer such illumination as we can in the darkness that surrounds us.

And make no mistake about it: we are surrounded by darkness. Though acts of kindness are everywhere and good people still give selflessly with no thought of reward, the sad

Kent Nerburn

fact is that children still starve, crimes are still visited upon the innocent, and the aged still spend their days afraid and isolated in lonely rooms. Whether we like it or not, families still wake to find their loved ones drowned on lonely and isolated beaches. Those who refuse to acknowledge this do no honor to the mystery and complexity of the world in which we live.

Francis's spiritual genius, and the source of his wisdom, is that he acknowledges this darkness while pointing to the light. He himself knew the darkness all too well. He was tormented by desires for the comforts of a wife and family. The streets he walked were teeming with beggars, and lepers thrust rotting limbs toward him in desperate attempts to get comfort and alms. His friars were imprisoned, pilloried, and beaten when they tried to proselytize in Germany. He himself was scorned when he tried to warn the leaders of the crusades about an impending slaughter and was reduced to weeping as his monks solemnly reported to him about the murder of the four thousand men whose deaths he had been powerless to prevent. Yet, in the face of all this and more, he never lost faith in the power of every individual to do good.

"Give light into the darkness," he said, and he went forth into the world to give such light as he could. For he knew that every bit of light, every small gesture, is needed. It is not our task to judge the worthiness of our own light or even to know if it is seen.

I often think of a moment in my son's school last year. His teacher, a kind and caring woman, was just packing up to leave for the weekend. Her day had been long, she was tired from a long bout with a chronic and debilitating illness, and she had company coming from out of town that evening. I had stopped to ask her a question, and we were talking briefly as she hurried to the door. Down the hall we saw a small child standing silently. It was one of her students—a young girl from a poor family who always came to school ragged and slightly sad. She followed bravely behind the other girls, but her clothing and her ineffable air of sadness set her apart. She was a child alone.

As we approached, the teacher looked at the girl. The little girl averted her eyes and said nothing. But instantly the teacher nodded me onward. She stopped in front of her student and knelt down so she was at the child's level and began talking quietly.

I continued down the hallway toward the door. Before I left I turned to see what was happening. The teacher had her hand on the child's shoulder, and they were casually walking back into the classroom. The little girl was talking animatedly, and the teacher was nodding, as if there was nothing else as important in the world as this child and the story she was telling.

Very likely that good woman went home that night completely exhausted, with no sense that she had done anything of significance. To her this was just an ordinary action of an ordinary day; she had simply been doing her job. And, if I know her as well as I think I do, she may even have berated herself for not being totally present to that child, for allowing her exhaustion to overtake her and her mind to wander to the obligations of that coming evening. Far from feeling that she had done any good by her small gesture, she may have gone to bed that evening feeling that she had failed to meet the responsibilities that had been placed before her in the course of the day.

But who is to say that the moment she spent shining light into that child's darkness was not every bit as significant as the time I spent with that poor bereft family on that Mexican beach? Who is to say that the touch she gave to that child did not unalterably change that child's life and thus affect the lives of all those with whom that young girl will come in contact in the course of her days?

The world is a strange and mysterious membrane. In the physics of human affairs our actions set off other actions that reverberate far beyond our vision, beyond even our capacity to predict or imagine. We have no more cause to judge the significance of our own actions than we have to judge the worthiness of those who receive them.

We are too quick to measure our lives by the dramatic moments, too ready to minimize the light that we shine into the small darknesses of everyday life. I will always be thankful for that opportunity of selfless service that was given me that morning in Mexico. But my true spiritual legacy on this earth may lie in a kind or harsh word, long forgotten, that I spoke in a chance meeting with a person I will never see again or in a moment that I spent, or failed to spend, with a lonely and friendless child. It is, after all, the least of our brothers and sisters that we are called to serve. It may be in the least of our moments that our greatest service lies.

If we chance upon a moment, such as that morning on the beach in Mexico, when all the skills at our command are called forth in a selfless gesture of service, and we are given the gift to shine light into a deep darkness, we should count ourselves blessed. But we are no less blessed, and no less called, when we are asked to bring a faint ray of hope, a small flicker of goodness, into the grayness of a young child's day.

We are not saints, we are not heroes. Our lives are lived in the quiet corners of the ordinary. We build tiny hearth fires, sometimes barely strong enough to give off warmth. But to the person lost in the darkness, our tiny flame may be the road to safety, the path to salvation.

It is not given us to know who is lost in the darkness that surrounds us or even if our light is seen. We can only know that against even the smallest of lights, darkness cannot stand.

A sailor lost at sea can be guided home by a single candle. A person lost in a wood can be led to safety by a flickering flame. It is not an issue of quality or intensity or purity. It is simply an issue of the presence of light.

This beautiful prayer reminds us that we all have light, no matter how faint and fragile, and it calls us to proceed as if it is our light that matters. Perhaps, it tells us, it is our light that will make a difference. Perhaps it will light up the dark corners of a young girl's life. Perhaps it will even help to lead a stranger home.

7

And where there is sadness, joy

There was a time in my life twenty years ago when I was driving cab for a living. It was a cowboy's life, a gambler's life, a life for someone who wanted no boss, constant movement, and the thrill of a dice roll every time a new passenger got into the cab.

What I didn't count on when I took the job was that it was also a ministry. Because I drove the night shift, the car became a rolling confessional. Passengers would climb in, sit behind me in total darkness and anonymity, and tell me of their lives.

We were like strangers on a train, the passengers and I, hurtling through the night, revealing intimacies we would never have dreamed of sharing during the brighter light of day.

In those hours, I encountered people whose lives amazed me, ennobled me, made me laugh, and made me weep. And none of those lives touched me more than that of a woman I picked up late on a warm August night.

I was responding to a call from a small brick fourplex in a quiet part of town. I assumed I was being sent to pick up some partyers or someone who had just had a fight with a lover or someone going off to an early shift at some factory in the industrial part of town.

When I arrived at the address, the building was dark except for a single light in a ground-floor window. Under these circumstances many drivers would just honk once or twice, wait a short minute, then drive away. Too many bad possibilities awaited a driver who went up to a darkened building at two-thirty in the morning.

But I had seen too many people trapped in a life of poverty who depended on the cab as their only means of transportation. Unless a situation had a real whiff of danger, I always went to the door to try to find the passenger. It might, I reasoned, be someone who needed my assistance. Would I not want a driver to do the same if my mother or father had called for a cab?

So I walked to the door and knocked.

"Just a minute," answered a frail and elderly voice. I could hear the sound of something being dragged across the floor.

After a long pause, the door opened. A small woman, somewhere in her eighties, stood before me. She was wearing a print dress and a pillbox hat with a veil pinned on it, like you might see in a costume shop or a Goodwill store or in a 1940s movie. By her side was a small nylon suitcase. The sound had been her dragging it across the floor.

The apartment looked as if no one had lived in it for years. All the furniture was covered with sheets. There were no clocks on the walls, no knickknacks or utensils on the counters. In the corner was a cardboard box filled with photos and glassware.

"Would you carry my bag out to the car?" she said. "I'd like a few moments alone. Then, if you could come back and help me? I'm not very strong."

I took the suitcase to the cab, then returned to assist the woman. She took my arm, and we walked slowly toward the curb. She kept thanking me for my kindness.

"It's nothing," I told her. "I just try to treat my passengers the way I would want my mother treated."

"Oh, you're such a good boy," she said. Her praise and appreciation were almost embarrassing.

When we got into the cab, she gave me an address, then asked, "Could you drive through downtown?"

"It's not the shortest way," I answered.

"Oh, I don't mind," she said. "I'm in no hurry. I'm on my way to a hospice."

I looked in the rearview mirror. Her eyes were glistening.

"I don't have any family left," she continued. "The doctor said I should go there. He says I don't have very long."

I quietly reached over and shut off the meter. "What route would you like me to go?" I asked.

For the next two hours we drove through the city. She showed me the building where she had once worked as an elevator operator. We drove through the neighborhood where she and her husband had lived when they had first been married. She made me pull up in front of a furniture warehouse that had once been a ballroom where she had gone dancing as a girl. Sometimes she would have me slow down in front of a particular building or corner and would sit staring out into the darkness, saying nothing.

As the first hint of sun was creasing the horizon, she suddenly said, "I'm tired. Let's go now."

We drove in silence to the address she had given me. It was a low building, like a small convalescent home, with a tar driveway that passed under a portico. Two orderlies came out to the cab as soon as we pulled up. Without waiting for me, they opened the door and began assisting the woman. They were solicitous, intent, watching her every move. They must have been expecting her; perhaps she had phoned them right before we left.

I opened the trunk and took the small suitcase up to the door. The woman was already seated in a wheelchair.

"How much do I owe you?" she asked, reaching into her purse.

"Nothing," I said.

"You have to make a living," she answered.

"There are other passengers," I responded.

Almost without thinking, I bent over and gave her a hug. She held on to me tightly. "You gave an old woman a little moment of joy," she said. "Thank you."

There was nothing more to say. I squeezed her hand once, then walked out into the dim morning light. Behind me I could hear the door shut. It was the sound of the closing of a life.

I did not pick up any more passengers that shift. I drove aimlessly, lost in thought. For the remainder of that day, I could hardly talk. What if that woman had gotten a driver who had been angry or abusive or impatient to end his shift? What if I had refused to take the run or had honked once, then driven away? What if I had been in a foul mood and had refused to engage the woman in conversation? How many other moments like that had I missed or failed to grasp?

We are so conditioned to think that our lives revolve around great moments. But great moments often catch us unawares. When that woman hugged me and said that I had brought her a moment of joy, it was possible to believe that I had been placed on earth for the sole purpose of providing her with that last ride. I do not think that I have ever done anything in my life that was any more important.

When Francis tells us to bring joy where there is sadness, it seems like a command that is out of balance. It is fair to ask us to bring solace where there is sadness or to provide comfort where there is sadness. But to bring joy seems to be too much to ask.

We tend to forget that sadness is like an empty room, filled with the gloom that covers everything like a shroud. It closes down the heart and envelops us in a dreary isolation. Try as we might, we can't escape. The efforts of our friends to bring us consolation seem distant and unreal. We appreciate them, but they do not touch the core of our isolation. We live inside a sepulchre of the spirit.

When, for a brief moment, someone is able to break through and touch us, it seems like a ray of sunlight that fills our entire heart. We know, in that moment, that we are alive and that our heart will heal.

To the bringer, it seems like no more than consolation. But to the person wrapped in the shroud of sadness, it feels more like joy. It is the affirmation and connection that reunites them with the human family.

How are we to know what act will bring this reconnection? Will it be a kind word? A bouquet of flowers? A short walk or conversation? Or maybe a crosstown ride in a cab?

Kent Nerburn

Almost always, it is something small. Those lost in a deep sadness will not assent to great efforts. They are too bound to the sadness that engulfs them. But they will permit the small acts. And though these small acts may seem like nothing to the giver, they have the possibility of being the miraculous touch that heals.

Francis, in all of Christianity, and maybe all of organized religion, is the greatest proponent of joy. He understood, better than any other, the power that it has to heal a heart.

When he calls us to sow joy where there is sadness, he is reminding us that a person engulfed in sadness is trapped in a prison of self-referential loneliness. It may seem that the highest act we can perform is to try to enter that prison and share the sadness. And, indeed, that may be the way to unlock the door to the isolated heart.

But to help that heart come forth from the darkness we must somehow bring in light from the outside. We must not only enter the room of their sadness; we must also hold the door open so that light can shine in.

Under normal circumstances, I might have sat with that woman who was, quite literally, going off to die. I might have tried to console her and empathize with her and make her feel less alone. It would have been a good gesture and a kind one. But because I was on a job, I could not embrace her loneliness and try to enter into it. I had to acknowledge it with a gentle touch, but I had to stay present to the outside world.

Though I did not know it at the time, I was doing the very thing that Francis counseled. It was only after she hugged me and spoke those poignant words that I began to understand.

We must remind ourselves that consolation is but the first step in healing. It is our way of saying that we share or, at least, honor another person's sadness. But healing has not truly taken place until the person lays down the sadness and returns to the fullness of life.

If we would follow in the footsteps of Francis, we must look beyond consolation to joy and seek the small and unexpected gesture that can create that joy. We don't always get it right; often we will miss the mark entirely. But when we find the exact touch that brings light into the lonely room of another's sadness, we are being true artists of the spirit. We are creating joy where there is sadness and helping another's spirit burst forth into song.

8

O Divine Master

Several years ago I attended a wedding where the bride and groom had chosen the Prayer of Saint Francis as one of the readings. We in the audience were asked to join in its recitation as a way of sharing and bearing witness to the union. I was seated next to an old friend who has a strong and active spiritual life but does not profess a particular faith. He willingly joined in with the prayer, as did we all. But when it was over, he turned to me and whispered, "If only it didn't have all that 'Lord' and 'Divine Master' stuff."

I understood what he was saying, even sympathized a bit. There is something so feudal, so overtly hierarchical and archaic and male about those terms of address.

Still, I dismissed his comment. After all, I reasoned, it is not the addressing of God that is important in the prayer; it is the spiritual guidance and nourishment the prayer contains. But I could not shake the gnawing sense of discomfort I felt about what my friend had said. I was reminded of an experience from my youth, and the painful truth it taught me that I carry with me to this day.

I was about ten and just beginning to come to an awareness of myself apart from the innocence of childhood. I awoke early on a warm summer morning and bounded downstairs to the living room where my father was reading the newspaper. Ever since I could remember, my father had awakened before anyone else, made himself a pot of coffee, and stretched out on the couch to read the morning news. From the time I was about eight I had shared this ritual with him.

He would finish reading a section and hand it to me. I would spread it out on the living room carpet and lie on my stomach with my hands propping up my chin, and we would read together in silence until it was time for him to get ready for work.

I loved this time together. It was the two men of the house sharing a moment of unspoken closeness. It made me feel proud, and it made me feel like a man.

But on this morning, something strange happened. I ran downstairs in my usual fashion. And, as usual, my father

Kent Nerburn

was reclining on the couch in the living room, reading the paper.

"Good morning, son," he said, handing me the sports section.

I started to respond as I always did. "Hi . . . ," I said.

But the next word did not come out. I had always called my father "Daddy," but now the word stuck in my mouth. It seemed too embarrassing, too much the province of the child.

All my life, up to that time, I had happily and comfortably addressed him as "Daddy." Suddenly, in one moment of awareness, everything changed. There before me, smiling at me with a father's love, was a man for whom I had no name.

If my father noticed, he did not say anything. I took the paper, and we read together until it was time for him to go to work. All seemed perfectly normal. But, inside, my heart was breaking.

The same thing happened the next morning, and the morning after. Each day I anguished over what to do. I cursed the decision made in my early youth that had led me to use this term of address. Why hadn't I done like so many of my friends and begun calling my father "Dad" from a very early age? That was a name with some muscle in it, a name I would never outgrow. But, whether by my own choice or by someone else's, I had grown up calling my father "Daddy," and now, at age ten, I was trapped in a childhood I could not transcend.

I am sure I could have gone to my father and asked him what he wanted to be called, and I am sure that he would have answered, "Whatever you like." I am sure I simply could have changed my manner of addressing him, and he would have smiled inwardly at my efforts to take a more adult role in relationship to him. But I did neither. Instead, I withdrew from any form of address and avoided ever having to call to him in a manner that required me to use a name for him.

To all outward appearances, nothing was different. We still did the same things together; we still talked in the same way. But, without knowing it, in that moment of awareness at age ten, something changed in our relationship. At that moment, in some fundamental way, I lost my father.

Over the years I found other ways to address him—the more formal "Father," the more jocular "Pop"—but I never was able to reclaim the intimacy of the relationship that had been mine when he had been "Daddy." Somewhere, in the name, in the nature of the address, there had been a truth that, once abandoned, was lost forever.

Those of us who have become uncomfortable addressing God as "Lord" or "Father" face a similar dilemma. We wake up one day uncomfortable with the form of address that we were given. "God" itself seems too formal and distant. "Father" sticks in our throats, especially if we are uncomfortable with the idea of God as male, or as having any gender at all.

We try on other names—the Great Spirit, the Great Mystery, Gaia, Ultimate Concern. But each is less satisfying than the last. They are all too forced or too theological or too vague or too something. They may be more inclusive, but they are less intimate. We have lost the name of God and have found nothing with which to replace it.

Gradually, like a ten-year-old boy uncomfortable with the name by which he was trained to address his father, we turn away from any form of direct address and try to continue our relationship without the delicious intimacy that comes from knowing how to address God by name.

This may not seem like much. But what we have lost is precious beyond all measure. For the further we move from the intimacy and closeness of a personal friendship, the more we reduce God to a philosophical principle. And in reducing God to a philosophical principle, in some indefinable way, we lose God.

To be sure, there are traditions that believe we must break the bonds of the human mind and get beyond the shaping of God in any fashion. For them, the experience of God is so great that it should require no name; indeed, it is beyond even thought and understanding.

But cannot a God who is beyond thought and understanding, who rides upon the stars and the winds and stretches beyond the edges of our dreams, also be capable of intimacies too impossible to believe?

The shape of the spiritual vessel we create to receive God will determine the shape of the God we experience. If we want to create a vessel that allows us to experience God as a loving, caring, active force in the world—one who knows our loves and fears and doubts and dreams—we need to be able to call our God by name.

For whether we like it or not, naming has a power. It is by naming that we learn the world around us and give shape to the infinite variety of experience. It is our way of defining, of claiming, of establishing a link between us and that which we have named.

If we have no name for God, no matter how paltry and distorting it may seem, we have no language by which to draw near to God as a caring and approachable Being.

I remember hearing a sermon once where the priest said that when Jesus used the word "Abba" to address God, as he did in the Lord's Prayer and in his lonely cry from the cross, he was not really using the word for "Father," but the word for "Dad" or "Daddy." At first this put me off. It seemed arch and contrived—the breezy sermonizing of a "happy talk" preacher. Most of all, it flew in the face of the unquestioned sense of formal distance and respect that I had been taught in my religious training. God was "Father," and to see God as "Dad" seemed bizarre. But I could not shake the sense of exhilaration that such a closeness offered. And when I later learned that the priest had been right, my heart was opened to a possibility of closeness with God that stays with me even to this day.

Most of us want this closeness to God. We want to know God as alive in our life, and our life as something alive in God. We may be uncomfortable with Francis's medieval way of addressing God as "Lord" and "Master," but this only means that we must find a different name by which to draw near.

There is no shame in admitting that when we name God we are framing our understanding of God by analogy and metaphor. Those are the only real tools we have to approach the unapproachable. This does not speak to a diminution of the Divine Mystery, only to the humble means of understanding that we have at our command.

Better that we should remember the cautionary tale of Augustine at the seashore, where he, in his wisdom, was said to have come upon a young child digging a hole in the sand and pouring water into it.

"What are you doing?" Augustine asked.

"I'm going to put the whole of the sea into this hole," the child replied.

"That's impossible," Augustine laughed.

"No more so," the child replied, "than your attempt to put the whole of God into the human mind."

When we give a name to God, we are saying that though we may not be able to fit God into the human mind, it is possible to fit God into the human heart.

And if our God is a living, caring presence who knows our deepest secrets and hears each time a sparrow falls, then ours is a God that is known through the heart and not through the mind.

If we would know this God, and not merely understand this God, we must have a name for God that we carry in our heart. For it is in the quiet of our heart that God will call our name. And when that call comes, should we not have a name with which to answer?

9

Grant that I may not seek so much to be consoled as to console

Today dawned hard and cold, with a chill around its heart. This morning word came that my nine-year-old son's best friend's mother had died.

It is not that her death was unexpected. She had been struggling against that dark force so feared by all women—the lump, so small and innocent, that grew, setting death loose into her blood and finally claiming her life. No, we all knew that her time was short. Despite the power of her spirit and the courage of her manner, the repeated hospitalizations, relapses, and growing fatigue reminded us constantly that her dying was a close and foreseeable event.

Still, when her death actually came, it struck us all a cruel and vicious blow. For we knew that in its wake a nine-year-old boy would be left standing by a graveside, forever separated from his mother and the innocent sunlit spaces of childhood.

She, too, had foreseen this, and it had broken her heart. How does one make peace with impending death when looking into the eyes of a young boy for whom you are the polestar, the mother, the source of all nourishment and love?

But, being a strong and private woman, she had made a choice from among the awful choices confronting her: she had chosen not to share her dying with her son, choosing instead to give him the precious gifts of her living so he would have the memory of her as a vibrant, caring woman rather than a dying one.

She masked and hid her illness, offering such normal reality as she could between the bouts of chemo and exhaustion. She made light of the lost hair, the unsteady gait. Until death claimed her, she was going to claim life and offer that only to her son.

It was a worthy choice, made with such lights as she had, and she had chosen it, I am sure, with the benefit of wise counsel and prayer. And it gave her son his mother, alive and vibrant, for as long as was humanly possible. But when her death came—and it came quickly—her son stood, shocked, cast in one moment into a foreign landscape from which he will never return.

Perhaps in the dim future he will understand and value the

gift of her strength and memories of a normal life. But now it only rings hollow in his heart, underscoring life's great betrayal and leaving him for all time with the echo of a scream where a mother's love ought to be.

My son, too, is terrified. His fear is everywhere, vague and unformed. His friend's mother was a mother to him, too. She was the one who took the children to the Saturday afternoon shows and bought them popcorn and whispered silly jokes. She was the one always ready to roast marshmallows or to hook up the hose for water fights or to pop a pizza in the oven. Just days ago he was at her house, oblivious to the darkness coursing through her veins, running past her on his way to play, taking her for granted in the way that children take their lives and parents for granted. Now he, too, is facing a void and is struggling to make sense of the unthinkable.

As I hold him close to me, I can feel the shudders of his body—the heaving sobs as he confronts his fears of my death, his own mother's death, death itself. Even his own mortality is no longer secure.

Now, at this young age, he is confronted by all the large questions for which there are no answers. Like his friend, he stands at the edge of the abyss, surrounded by toys and forts and bike rides and ball games, and stares into the incomprehensible face of death.

I want to comfort him. But what am I to tell him?

That death is a grinning thief, coming around unexpected corners? That if we have faith there is a better life waiting for us on the other side?

These may be true, but they offer no light on the darkness. I have no hidden knowledge that makes death more understandable, only the balm that I have lived, and in having lived, more willingly offer myself to its mystery.

He looks at me and sniffles. "Dad, there's two things about death that bother me," he says, searching for words. "The one I know is that death comes to everybody. The one I don't know is what it feels like to die."

I give him soothing answers about the beatific visions people have had when they have returned from clinical death. I speak in broad terms about the continuity of the spirit and the gentle embrace of God for which we all yearn. I say nothing about the tortured screams of people enslaved by pain, begging for release, or the words of a friend's father right before he passed: "What's happening to me? I don't understand. What's happening to me?"

I would love to illuminate this hidden landscape for him and to bathe it in a gentle light. But I cannot. I have no answers; I can only help him frame the questions and move gently toward an acceptance of that which none of us can avoid.

Then, almost like a gift, the words of Francis come back to me. "Grant that I may not seek so much to be consoled as to console."

What you must do now, I say, is console your friend. You must find a way to be with him. You cannot cross the line into his grief; you cannot find that place. Grief is like a stone in the water, plunging downward into darkness. The rings spread out from that center, touching us ever more lightly the further we are from that event.

"You are in the first ring outward for Danny," I tell him. "You loved Karen, too. Find a way to be there for him."

He looks up at me. "I feel sad for Danny and Karen. But I'm happy Mom isn't dead."

"I know," I answer. "It's okay."

The dark twists of the surviving soul are working their way through his psyche, and he cannot absorb them in a way that is understandable.

Death is a cruel trickster, robbing us of the purity of our grief. Who among us does not find at least the tiniest sliver of relief that the passing was not ours? Something below will, below consciousness, woven into the very fabric of the human animal, makes us claim the self, though we desperately want to meet the absolute of death with an absolute purity in our response. But we cannot. In secret corners we dare not reveal, we celebrate our own survival. It is the will of the species, seeking to advance and perpetuate itself by making us choose life even in the face of an absolute such as death.

Only in the act of consoling can we find purity, for only the desire to console comes unalloyed with feelings of self-congratulation or relief or guilt. It, too, is something woven into the species—to bear witness to the passing of another and to bow our heads at the mystery it contains. Even the animals gather around one of their own who has died, and in their brute fashion they, too, mourn and console. Perhaps this is what Francis saw that made him look upon them as brothers and sisters.

It's all right, I tell my son, to have a sense of relief. We all celebrate a little when the dark angel passes. What you must do now is to console Danny in the way that feels best. Maybe you can hug him; maybe you can talk to him. Maybe you can just be there with him. Give what you can to make him know that he isn't alone.

My son swallows deeply. He is taking the words, the thought, into himself. He seems so small standing there—so alone, so unsuited to the task at hand.

What will he do?

Perhaps he is not given to greatness of heart; it is not a gift granted to all equally.

Perhaps he cannot find the caring to move beyond his fear of death and can do no more than stand an uneasy and distant vigil.

Perhaps he may be able to enter closely into his friend's

pain and offer a bridge to life through the outpouring of his own love and kindness.

He will give whatever his heart is able, for he, like all of us, yearns to offer consolation. It is our way of holding the hands of those we love as they lean over the dark and unfathomable chasm of death.

I often think of the story of Francis meeting with the leper on the Umbrian plain. He was traveling alone on horseback when he came around a bend in the road and found himself face-to-face with a man disfigured by leprosy. Frail himself, and prone to illness, he was terrified of the sick and rotting man before him, and his first thought was to turn and flee.

But he did not.

He stepped down from his horse and tentatively walked toward the dying man, put his arms around him, and despite his nausea and repulsion, kissed the man's rotting fingers.

He did not do this easily. He did not even do it willingly. If purity of heart had been the measure of his act, it would have had no value at all, for he was filled with abhorrence and nausea at the man he saw before him. But the person in the darkness does not measure your light and does not look upon you as less if the act you performed was less than pure. What matters is that Francis did it. And in the doing of it the gift he gave to that leper was exceeded only by the gift he gave to himself.

I look at my son standing frightened before me. He, too, has come around a bend and is standing face-to-face with his own deepest fears and terrors. He does not need to be pure of heart. He merely needs to have the courage to do the most he can.

I say a silent prayer in my heart. "Let him be strong," I ask. "If he can reach out and touch this, so be it. If he can only stand near and bear witness, so be that as well. Just don't let him turn and flee."

The phone rings. It is Danny. My son walks over and picks up the receiver. He cups his hand around it as if to keep me from hearing what he says, but the room is small, and filled with the silence of our grief.

"Oh, Danny," he says, "I'm so sorry."

My heart almost bursts with pride, with sadness, with joy, at this small act of consolation, for with those words he has started two hearts on the long lonely path toward healing.

10

To be understood as to understand

"You don't understand me. Nobody understands me." It's a cry that comes from all of us at those moments when circumstances separate us from others or we feel too weary from trying and too unable to communicate the content of our hearts.

And it is probably true. No one does understand us. Though united by a common humanity, we are separated by our individuality. None of us can know for certain what goes on in the mind and heart of another.

When we feel this sense of isolation and being misunderstood, our natural inclination is to recede from the world and to hope that someone can reach across the chasm of our loneliness to establish the human contact that we so desperately desire.

But in his prayer, Saint Francis reminds us that the true way out of our loneliness is not to seek the balm of understanding from others but to try to reach across the chasm ourselves. It is in the act of trying to understand others, he reminds us, that the miracle of growth and creation lies.

I am often reminded of a story I once heard about an ordinary man from Oklahoma who became caught up in the great global tragedy of World War II.

He was an ordinary boy who had led an ordinary life. He had been raised in a small town, and when the call to war came, he, like so many others his age, had entered into the service of his country with no real preparation or sense of what this service would ultimately entail.

He enlisted in the navy, and though he had never even so much as been on a rowboat, his capacity for leadership was noticed, and he was ultimately given command of a ship. He acquitted himself honorably and did what was asked of him while the long, cruel war in the Pacific raged. And when the final Japanese surrender was announced, he and his men were assigned the task of pacifying some of the small islands in the South Pacific and returning the Japanese forces to their homes. One of these was the island of Truk.

The Japanese soldiers who were garrisoned on Truk had been led to believe that their surrender meant inevitable torture and murder at the hands of the American victors. They each mustered such courage as they were able in the face of this anticipated savagery and watched stoically as the American troops steamed into the harbor.

The Japanese major, a man of personal dignity and honor, had in his possession a samurai sword that had been given to him by his grandfather when he had graduated from the military academy. It had been in the family for generations and was the symbol and very embodiment of his sense of honor as a soldier. As the Americans landed, they walked up and shook the Japanese soldiers' hands. They offered them food and clothing and treated them with the utmost respect. All of this the Japanese major noted, and he attributed it to the integrity of the young commander in charge of the troops.

When it was time for the Japanese forces to be shipped back to Japan, the major approached the young American commander from Oklahoma who had treated his soldiers with such civility and handed over his samurai sword as a gesture of gratitude and honor.

The American took the sword and expressed his gratitude in response. As a child of the Oklahoma plains, the code of the Samurai meant little to him, and the sword was little more than one of those poignant mementos of warfare that victors tend to claim from the defeated. But he was unable to forget the look in the Japanese major's eyes, and he made a vow that someday he would return the sword to that man.

Years passed, and the sailor from Oklahoma made several inquiries about the Japanese major. But he did not have enough information to find the man, and so he let the matter drop.

It was only decades later, when his son was studying in Japan, that the American commander thought again about the possibility of returning the sword to its owner. Through the efforts of several Japanese officials, the son located the address of the now elderly major. He passed this address on to his father in Oklahoma, and the process was set in motion by which the sword would be returned to the man and his family.

It took several months, but the connection was made. The sword was delivered to Japan, where the major received it, in his own words, as if a son who he had long thought was dead suddenly walked through the front door.

Over the next several years the two men who had been linked by that sword corresponded and opened the best of their hearts to each other. They shared their memories of the past and their hopes for the future. They exchanged stories of their families and stories of their lives. Over the common legacy of that sword, they became friends.

The man from Oklahoma dreamed of meeting his Japanese friend face-to-face, but he was ill and not able to travel. So his family arranged that, on the day of the annual family reunion, the Japanese major would arrive at the small

Kent Nerburn

Oklahoma restaurant where the reunion was being held and surprise his American friend.

At the reunion, as the annual familial greetings were being exchanged, the son announced that there was a special surprise awaiting his father. Major Tohata, the man to whom he had returned the sword, was outside the door. Major Tohata came in, and the two men embraced. Tears flowed, and the lives of two ordinary men came full circle before the eyes of the ordinary Oklahoma citizens who were blessed to witness the event. In that moment, the struggles of a half century of the human spirit had their resolution in a single, tearful embrace.

The sailor from Oklahoma died not long after that meeting. But his life's work on this earth had been realized in the return of that sword and the embrace of that enemy turned friend. No one who was present at the event or who was touched by it at a distance has ever again been quite as hard of heart or quite as doubting about the capacity of the human spirit for love and understanding.

What that ordinary man from Oklahoma did was to use the circumstances he had been given in life to create understanding. He could easily have retreated and used the experience of the war to isolate him from others who had not shared the experience. A great many soldiers do so, saying, "You don't understand. You just can't understand." They wrap themselves in the incommunicability of their wartime experience, and use it as a reason to wall themselves off from others.

But the man from Oklahoma took the opposite path—the path that the prayer of Francis counsels. He did not seek to be understood but only to understand. He looked in the eyes of a man who had been sworn to kill him and did not see "enemy" but saw "brother." And then he acted on what he had seen, entering into the mind and heart of that other man to try to understand what this simple blade of metal might have meant to him.

By the time he had followed out the thread of that first moment of trying to understand, he had created a meaning in the world that had stretched across an ocean and embraced people on two continents. And in doing so, he had revealed himself in a way that made him forever understood by those whose lives he touched.

That is the miracle of seeking to understand. When we try to understand another, we reveal ourselves, and in revealing ourselves we are able to be understood. Our heart declares itself to another heart, and that which is common between us becomes the bridge over which understanding crosses.

It is so easy to look upon understanding as an uncovering of patterns and principles. We see it as some passive condition that will descend upon us through the application of our own intellect. But what passive application of his intellect would have provided that ordinary man from Oklahoma with an understanding of the reasons of war? What possible system of analysis would have begun to approach the understanding that he gained by actively seeking to create meaning out of the circumstances that he had been given?

We must remind ourselves that, though our lives are small and our acts seem insignificant, we are generative elements of this universe, and we create meaning with each act that we perform or fail to perform.

It is here, on this earth, in the day to day, on the street corners, at our evening table, in the homes of our friends, at the bedside of the sick, in the arms of our wife or husband, in the warmth or sadness of our child's days, that the universe is being formed.

Far from being a great system and puzzle that we are asked to comprehend, it is a dynamic, ever-changing reality that we can influence by our every act and gesture.

If we choose to see our individuality as isolation, we draw back from the acts that make a difference, and we wait passively to be understood. But if, instead, we choose to see our individuality as uniqueness, we realize that the circumstances of our own tiny lives present us with occasions of influence that will never come to anyone else, and we reach out with courage to create understanding by performing the acts that no one else will ever have the opportunity to perform.

The man from Oklahoma could have allowed the giving of the sword to become an act of insignificance. He could have accepted the sword, taken it home to Oklahoma, and hung it on a wall in his basement to serve as a conversation piece for his grandchildren. But he did not. Instead, he made it an act of great significance by his actions in response to the gift. And the actions he performed were driven by the fact that he sought to understand rather than to be understood.

In some small way, every day each of us is handed a sword by another. It may be an actual object; it may be a conversation. It may be given in anger; it may be given in gratitude. It may even seem like nothing in the giving. But it is a part of another person's life, and something in who we are or the circumstances we share makes the giving a significant part of our small role in shaping the universe.

If we ignore it or denigrate it or appropriate it for ourselves with no thought of what it meant to the other person, we fail to take the full responsibility that we are granted for the creation of meaning in this universe. But if we reach across and try to understand the reason why this person, in this circumstance, has chosen to act in this particular way, we start a process of dynamic involvement that can reverberate across time and space in ways that we cannot even imagine.

That young soldier from Oklahoma may not have thought that he was performing an act of great significance. He may not have had even the slightest inkling of the true meaning of that sword to the Japanese major. But in responding to the circumstances of his own ordinary life with an extraordinary effort at understanding, he created meaning that bridged an ocean and gave hundreds, maybe thousands, of people a glimpse into the most noble part of the human spirit.

If an ordinary man from Oklahoma can stand against the horrors of war with only a samurai sword and a quest for understanding, who are we to think that our actions are too insignificant to have an effect in this world?

11

To be loved as to love

Years ago, while studying sculpture, I lived in the Italian city of Florence for several months. Often, when the days were hot, I would seek out the cool quiet of the cathedrals and museums and stand before the great masterworks that graced almost every surface and corner of that amazing city.

Though many artists thrilled me, it was Giotto who fascinated me. His work seemed to balance on the very cusp of the Middle Ages and the Renaissance. His figures still had the iconographic stillness of players in a great theological drama, but in their hands and faces were the first stirrings of individuality and personality. Truly, these were the servants of God, but they were also possessed of human feelings and consciousness. I could look into their eyes and see a sister or brother across the great divide of time.

Among my favorite works by Giotto were the frescoes in the church of Santa Croce, and my favorite among them was the fresco depicting the funeral of Saint Francis. It showed the saint on his funeral bier surrounded by mourners with their hands raised in gestures of solemn benediction and their faces frozen into emblems of all-too-human grief.

But on Francis's face Giotto had painted a smile of almost ineffable peace. It was subtle and delicate—more a fragrance than a look—as if the saint knew a secret that not even death could contain.

I would sketch that face for hours, trying to discover the key that would unlock the secret of that smile.

Often, while I was working, I would overhear the conversations of other visitors. German, French, Italian, Japanese, Iranian, Turkish, American, Pakistani—every nationality, every religious persuasion came through to view the frescoes. And though most of them had come for the spiritual and aesthetic brilliance of Giotto, very often their conversations would move from the art itself to the subject that it was meant to depict: the life and character of Francis of Assisi.

Over the course of months, I began to hear the same thoughts expressed: "He was the saint who loved the animals." "He was the privileged son who gave away everything he owned and stood naked before his father." "He was the one who preached to the birds." "He was the gentle saint."

The knowledge was not always accurate. Often it was apocryphal. But it was clear that Saint Francis, God's Little Poor One, had captured the hearts and imaginations of people from all around the world, and they all—whether Christian, Jew, atheist, agnostic, Buddhist, Jain, Hindu, or Muslim—saw in him a flowering of spiritual purity that filled them with admiration and love.

What was it, I asked myself, about this simple Italian man that so transcended the boundaries of faith and belief and made so many take him to their hearts as one of their own?

Then one day, while leaving the church, I had a glimpse of an answer.

As I stepped forth into the daylight, I saw a young couple walking—almost skipping—hand in hand across the piazza. They were laughing and singing, obviously deeply in love. Occasionally they would stop and feed the pigeons or say something to a tourist sitting on a bench. Occasionally they would lovingly touch each other's face or share a tiny kiss.

Their love was so pure and infectious that even the old women going to the cathedral for Mass would smile at them as they passed. The young couple reminded them of something in their youth, and they remembered it as good.

At that moment I realized what it is that makes Francis so beloved to so many. He always acted like a man who had just fallen in love, and all of us, of any faith, any age, any nationality, remember that as good.

Falling in love is the secret dream that lives inside each of our hearts. It is the human expression of our deepest yearning for union, our desire to have the walls that separate us from others broken down.

When we fall in love, the whole world is suddenly suffused with a glow that our heart has never experienced. It is as if we had been living beneath a cloud, and now, for the first time, the sun has burst forth in all its glory.

We feel connected to everything; all creatures are our brothers and sisters. We want to run through the streets laughing and singing and hugging everyone we meet.

It is the closest many of us ever come to feeling holy.

The magic of Francis is that his holiness always felt like fresh love. He would burst into song in the middle of a public square; he spoke with birds and fishes; he picked up worms and carried them to the side of the road to keep them from being crushed underfoot.

Everything on earth and in the heavens—the stars, the animals, the sun and moon—was his brother and sister. He felt connected to all living things, and nothing, whether a tree or a pool of water or a leper or a wild beast in the woods, was too insignificant for his concern. He danced through the world embracing everything he saw.

How close this is to the innocent joy of love, and how much it warms the hearts of all of us who have known a first love's blessing. Like the old women hobbling across the piazza of Santa Croce and glancing at the young lovers, we cannot help but smile when we are in the presence of Francis's joyous and loving faith.

One of the most wonderful stories that has come down to us about Francis is of the winter he spent at the hermitage on the mountainside in Sarteano. One evening he had retired to his cell to pray when suddenly everything became too much for him. He was overcome by a deep loneliness and hopelessness about his celibate lifestyle, and he was sorely tempted to give it all up.

At first he tried to mortify himself physically. But when that didn't work he arrived at a solution that only he could have devised. He rushed out, half clothed, onto the winter hillside and feverishly began building a row of seven snowmen.

After he finished he stood back and began speaking.

"There you are, Francis," he said out loud. "The family you want is complete."

He pointed to one of the snowmen. "This is your wife."

Then he pointed to four smaller snowmen. "These are the four children she has given you, two sons and two daughters."

Pointing to the last two, he said, "These are your servant and maid. But they are all naked and cold. Now hurry and get them something to wear before they freeze to death."

Pausing a moment, he addressed himself again. "What? You hesitate? You say there are too many of them? Then remain in God's service, friend, and don't think about anything else."

Is there another person of any faith who would have met a dark night of the soul by building a family of snowmen?

But this was pure and essential Francis. Overcome by unutterable loneliness, he did not yearn for someone to love him. Instead, he yearned for someone he could love. It is as if the idea of needing to be loved never crossed his mind. His heart cried out not to receive love but to give it.

This is the lesson he offers us when he tells us to seek to love rather than to be loved. Love, he is telling us, is something indwelling in our hearts. It only comes alive by being given.

If we feel ourselves surrounded by loneliness, our first act should not be to call out for someone to love us but to seek out someone or something on which to lavish our love. Only then will we break down the barriers of our own sense of isolation.

For him, this was a way of life. But never did he express it more purely than during the harsh winter that he and his monks passed in an abandoned hut near a stream called Rivo Torto.

It was an especially difficult time for the monks. The quarters were so cramped that they were barely able to all fit inside at the same time, and the rations were so poor that they were reduced to eating rotting turnips they found lying in the field.

One night one of the monks began moaning.

"I'm dying, I'm dying," he groaned.

Francis got up from his place on the floor and went to the aid of the man.

"What do you think you're dying of, Brother?" he asked.

"I'm dying of hunger," the monk answered.

Immediately, Francis bade all the other monks to rise and set the table. Then he brought forth such food as they had and spread it before them, and they all ate together, so the monk who had been moaning would not be ashamed of his hunger.

Could there be a more beautiful expression of the selfless nature of love? Francis did not criticize; he did not judge. If he felt dismayed at the monk's weakness, he did not show it. Neither did he act because he wanted praise or recognition or because his heart was empty and needed to be filled. He did this simply because he was filled with love for his hungry brother and wanted to honor and protect him. And we can only imagine the love that the monk felt in return for this gentle man who had hidden his weakness rather than exposing it.

In this small gesture, Francis reveals the miracle of a love that is given with no thought of return.

By loving the hungry monk in all his weakness, Francis brought forth the love in the monk's heart. And all who saw Francis's gesture were bathed in the presence of that love as well, because they could not help but feel the gentle purity and affection with which it was offered.

Love that was given became love that was received and, once received, was given again. It increased and multiplied and spread out among the monks and from there across the world, until it touches us today as we place the story in our hearts. And it will touch others in the future when we recount the story to them or when we try to live a life that follows the path of Francis's example.

All this because one man chose to give love when he was able to do so rather than waiting for love to be given.

Such a teaching this is about love's gentle truths.

Love is active and generative. Its seed must be planted if it is to grow.

Love has no judgment; it is not conditional. It asks no recognition; it demands no response. Its reward is in its giving, but it has no thought of reward. It reaches out to those around it, not because they are deserving or because they can offer something in return, but because they are part of God's creation, and all of creation is worthy of our love.

The empty heart that seeks to receive love rather than give it is like a constricting container in which the roots of love cannot spread. It tries to define love and make it take the shape of its need.

But love that is given takes root where it will, and its branches spread out to shelter those around it. And as its seeds fall, new love grows and the cycle of love begins anew.

It all seems so simple, so obvious. But too often we forget these truths.

When we are feeling weak we seek love. When we are feeling strong we husband our love and dole it out according to the measure in which we feel it is deserved. Only when we are filled to overflowing with love, like that young couple on the piazza of Santa Croce, do we spread our love unconditionally across all of creation.

But in his life and his words, Francis reminds us that love we give, no matter why or in what measure it is given, will be returned to us a thousandfold. It will fill the vessel of our own need and will spread out across the world like ripples on the water, reaching places we neither dream nor imagine. We need only trust that it must first be given, and all else will be revealed.

Often, when I feel a lack of love or a hardness of spirit, I try to place myself among children. Their hearts are pure, and their ways are guileless. They offer me a clear window into the human heart.

The other day I was in a schoolroom with a young girl who was playing with a group of stuffed animals. She was talking to them and holding them and engaging them in imaginary conversation. She sang softly to them as she played.

I watched her lift these little animals to her face, kiss them, and whisper gently in their ears. She was showering them with her love.

She did not care that the animals could not love her back; it was enough that she could love them. Like Francis, she simply wanted a family she could love.

I went home that night with a warmth in my heart, and I thought of my own family, imperfect in its shape, struggling in its ways. I thought of my stepdaughters and stepson, for whom I have always tried to be a parent without stealing away the role of their father. I looked at my son, who has grown now to an age where I must loose the embrace in which I so dearly want to hold him. I watched my wife, one with me and yet a person in her own right, with her own dreams and fears and private cares. And I realized that like the little girl, like Francis, I, too, simply wanted a family I could love and that from them I wanted nothing in return.

A smile crossed my lips. We were like God's snowmen—imperfect and transient, created by him solely so he could lavish us with his love.

The thought pleased me, and all evening the smile stayed with me.

Even as I lay in my bed waiting for sleep, the smile would not leave me. And though I could not see it, I recognized it, for I knew it in my heart.

It was the same smile that Giotto had placed on the face of Francis, the same smile that I had seen on the old women as they looked upon the young lovers in the Piazza Santa Croce, the same smile that had graced the lips of the young girl as she sang softly to the stuffed animals. It was the smile of love overflowing, and I wanted to weep with joy for the blessing I had been given.

12

For it is in giving that we receive

The caring teacher who is overworked and driven to the point of exhaustion every day; the philanthropist who gives away large amounts of money with no thought of return; the volunteer who serves the needs of the sick or the indigent—all seem to be driven by a greatness of heart that eludes most of us in our daily lives. But ask them why they do it, and they will all give you the same answer: "I get more than I give."

At first glance this sounds like a platitude. But if we look more deeply, we discover that these people all know one of the great secrets of life: our spirits are nourished by giving, just as our bodies are nourished by food.

This is not mystical; it is not high-minded. It is a simple truth about the way that the energy of life flows back and forth between people when a moment of giving takes place.

I once had a friend who was an actor. He had been a long-time student of the craft, someone who, with the movement of a hand or the subtlest modulation of a voice, could create an entire world of meaning in a scene or a character. On one occasion he and I were sitting together discussing some issue about which I thought I had some deep insight. I was going on at great length about my thinking on the matter, when suddenly I lost my train of thought.

I looked over at him sheepishly. "I forgot what I was saying," I said.

"I know," he answered. "It's because I wasn't listening."

He, who understood the subtle connections between human beings better than anyone I have ever met, knew that giver and receiver are bound to each other in ways that most of us can never imagine.

Since that day I have watched this occurrence hundreds of times in conversations. Whether it is the subtle cues of the response of the listener or something deeper and more psychic, I can't stay. But I know that my friend spoke the truth. It is the emotional and spiritual presence of the listener that gives the speaker focus and energy.

Ask any person who speaks before audiences or who gives

Kent Nerburn

public performances on an instrument, and they will tell you the same thing. There is something in the connection between the person offering and the person receiving that either kills a moment or brings that moment alive.

When true giving takes place, something new and alive is created in the space between the giver and the one who receives. Two people who moments before had no real connection suddenly open themselves to each other—the one by offering something of value, the one by having the goodness of heart to accept—and in the space between something magical is created. Neither can predict what this will be, but both will benefit, and often it is the giver who benefits most.

Once again I am reminded of that most pivotal moment in Francis's young life, when he came around the bend on the Umbrian plain and found himself face-to-face with the leper. When he dismounted his horse, walked to the leper that so horrified him, and kissed the man's oozing and suppurating fingers, it was he who was doing the giving, but it was he who received the most. In a way he never expected, he was filled with happiness and joy, and from that moment, he went forth into the world performing acts of giving and charity whenever and wherever he could.

The leper, too, received much. In his lonely and wretched isolation, he received what we all need most—the gift of another's touch. That kiss and embrace from Francis affirmed in him that he was more than just his disease; he was part of the human family. Even if his heart had become so hard that he did not see Francis's act as a gift, he had nonetheless been touched, and at that touch his rotting body had to rejoice.

In the gift of his embrace, Francis sent two men forward in their lives richer, fuller, and more at peace for the moment they had shared. Through his act of giving, he had created meaning where before there had been none. And in doing so, he had added something new to the richness and fullness of creation.

We must never underestimate the power of giving and what it can do for our hearts. When we give, we are opening the doors of possibility in a way that allows the light of love to shine through. And in that light, miracles can occur.

I remember a situation when I was teaching a class in religious art at a seminary. The head of the school came to me one day and said, "I have a student I don't know what to do with. He wants to be a juggler and have that be his ministry. We have no one who can teach him. Perhaps you might consider working with him."

I protested that I knew nothing about juggling but agreed to meet with the young man.

When he arrived I saw a person filled with hope and possibility who was possessed of an impossible dream. I agreed to work with him, but only under certain conditions.

"I can't teach you anything about juggling," I told him.

Kent Nerburn

"You will have to learn that for yourself. But I might be able to help you learn how your juggling can be a gift to this world. If I agree to work with you, you must promise never to let me see you juggle until the last day of the class, and in between, you must do everything I say."

The young man, whose name was Philip, agreed, and we set about the task of framing a learning experience for him. We read the story of the clown of God; we studied Francis as "the fool for Christ." We spoke of the tradition of the jester and read the diaries of famous clowns. But none of this satisfied him. "I don't want to learn about history," he told me. "I want to find a ministry."

The next week, when he arrived, I opened the Bible to the fifth chapter of Matthew and pointed to the Beatitudes.

"Read these," I told him. "From now on, each week you will go out on the streets and juggle one of the blessings. You cannot speak, you cannot explain to anyone what you are doing. You must decide for yourself how and where you are to do this, and you must do it with a pure heart. At the end of each week we will get together, and you will tell me which Beatitude you juggled, how you did it, and what you have learned."

Being an adventurous sort and filled with wonder at the richness of human experience, Philip immediately agreed. For the next nine weeks he went forth into the heart of the city with his little sack of red balls and tried to give voice to the Beatitudes through the silent testimony of his juggling.

He juggled in nursing homes, he juggled at the jail, he juggled on the street, he juggled in people's homes. His adventures were humorous, harrowing, and heartbreaking. One man gave him his coat; in a group home for retarded adults he was surrounded and hugged by all the residents. One night he was beaten by a bunch of thugs and had to get medical treatment. But still he persevered.

As the quarter drew to a close, he had only one Beatitude left to juggle: "Blessed are the poor in spirit, for theirs is the kingdom of heaven." "How am I to know who is poor in spirit?" he asked. "Where am I supposed to find them?"

"That's for you to decide," I told him. "Remember our agreement." He went away a bit downcast. I could tell he was getting weary, and I felt bad, thinking that perhaps I had asked too much of him.

But that Friday, when we were to meet to discuss what he had done that week, he burst into my office with a glow around him that I had never seen before.

"You'll never believe what happened," he said. "I could hardly wait until today to tell you."

Breathlessly, he recounted the events of the week. He had gone to the city hospital, figuring that people who were in a hospital were in low spirits. He walked through the front door juggling his collection of balls. No one paid any attention as he got on the elevator and went up to an inpatient floor. He stepped off the elevator and nodded to the people at the nursing station, juggling all the while.

"Can we help you?" a woman asked.

Philip just smiled and kept on juggling.

"You aren't allowed on this floor unless there is someone you're visiting," she said. "Who are you here to see?"

Philip said nothing and began juggling his way down the corridor toward the patients' rooms.

The nurse called after him, "Who is it you're here to see? You can't be in here unless you're here to see someone in particular."

Still, he did not respond.

Apparently, at that point she sounded an alarm. Instantly, orderlies came running from all directions. They surrounded Philip and began to move toward him. "He must have gotten out of lockup," one said, referring to the psych ward on the fourth floor. "Sedate him and take him back up there."

Philip was terrified. He had long since ceased carrying a billfold when he juggled because of the threat of robbery and beatings. And it was rapidly becoming clear that even if he broke our agreement and spoke to explain himself, the nurse and the orderlies were not going to believe his story.

The orderlies moved closer.

He could not run. He could not escape. A nurse had gone to get the hypodermic and the sedative.

He stood against the wall, surrounded, juggling in fear, when an elderly man in his hospital gown came out of the door of a nearby room. He looked at Philip and the orderlies. "He's here to see me," he said. "Come on in. I've been waiting for you."

The orderlies looked confused. The nurses backed off.

"It's all right," said the man. "He's here for me." And he led Philip into his room. Then the man got back into his bed and gestured Philip to keep juggling.

For the next half hour Philip juggled like he never had in his life. The man lay there, propped up by his pillows, smiling, saying nothing, until Philip was done.

Then he applauded.

Philip picked up his juggling balls and stepped cautiously back into the corridor. The nurses stared at him. The orderlies stood by with arms folded as he passed. He smiled at them and made his way back down the elevator and out into the street without ever having said a single word.

He had never seen that man before. He did not know who he was or why he did what he did. He only knew that the man had saved him from a situation that could have resulted in something very ugly.

"What did you learn?" I asked him.

"The world is full of miracles," he answered. "And sometimes we get more than we give."

"I think you've found your ministry," I said. "Class dismissed."

When we take the chance of opening ourselves and giving, miraculous occurrences can indeed take place. It is not always easy; it usually involves risk. Francis did not know what would result when he decided to get down from his horse and embrace the leper. Philip did not know what would happen when he went out on the street to juggle the Beatitudes.

Neither do we know what will happen when we take a child into our home or listen to the story of someone we meet on a corner or give a quarter to a beggar or read stories in a nursing home. All we can be sure of is that there is the possibility of magic in the space between us and those to whom we give.

If we have the courage to trust in this magic and not see giving as some kind of a diminution of our own resources, we, like Francis, like Philip, like the teacher and the volunteer and the philanthropist, will learn one of the greatest secrets of life. We will learn that nothing we can ever give will compare with the gift we receive when a human heart says, "Come on in. I've been waiting for you." For in that moment, we will feel a touch upon our spirit that for all the world feels like a blessing from the hand of God.

13

It is in forgiving that we are forgiven

I have many friends who carry on their shoulders the harsh burden of anger at their parents. They have been steeped in the ways of psychology, and they see their own failures in life as a reflection of the twists and turns wrought upon them during their upbringing.

They may be right. The alcoholic father, quick with the strap, leaves scars that run far deeper than the skin. The mother who abandons her children or clings to them in an orgy of self-absorption puts chains on their hearts that can never be completely loosed.

Yet life is a gift, and each day a miracle. If we insist on dwelling on the flawed shape of our lives, we become blind to the beauty and mystery of the world around us.

All of us have been wronged; all of us have wronged another. In an indirect but very real way, we wrong the earth itself by living on it—we use its resources for our own needs and pleasure, take the lives of other species for our own sustenance. Yet we do no good by dwelling upon these wrongs. They are part of the act of living and simply show that we are engaged in the world in which we live.

If we would truly experience the miracle of life and the richness of each day, we must learn to forgive—ourselves, those around us, and those who have come before us, on whose shoulders, for better or for worse, we stand. It is the only way to clear our hearts and spirits so that we are open to the fullness and beauty of life.

Most people think of forgiveness as something that takes place in the space between people. And in many cases it is. But real forgiveness starts with the self, for until we can forgive ourselves, we can never see the world clearly enough to forgive others.

I will carry with me forever the memory of my father, for whom education was everything, trying to go back to college after he had retired from a lifetime spent working to support a family.

Tentatively, guardedly, he enrolled in a humanities course—a subject that had always fascinated him and about which he believed he had some understanding. Like the accurate and diligent man he was, he did all the readings, took all the notes, and approached every lecture with a great sense of preparation and serious-mindedness. For his final project he chose to do a paper on the history of the English language. He worked long and hard on the project, casting it in the form of a Socratic dialogue and investing it with all the creativity and diligence at his command.

I remember him calling me after he had handed it in. His voice was bursting with pride. The intellectual yearnings submerged for forty years were finally seeing the light of day. He could hardly wait for the response of the professor.

When he got the paper back, he found it covered with red-penciled margin notes and imperious comments. It apparently had landed in the hands of a graduate assistant, who had taken it upon himself to savage my father and his struggling efforts at academic style and expression.

My father said little but sent the paper out to me. I was the only member of the family who had ever graduated from college. I was working on my Ph.D. and was the one person he looked up to in terms of academic achievement. I was his only hope for salvaging such little pride and confidence as he had left.

I do not remember what exactly I said or did. I only know that I "regraded" the paper and made a new set of margin notes. I am sure I was guided by good intentions, but I am also sure that in my efforts to sound academic and professorial, I further destroyed my father's confidence and resolve.

He never took another course again.

My father is now dead. His single abiding passion in life was education. His greatest unfinished accomplishment in life was his undergraduate degree. And the one person who could have buoyed him up and spurred him on to get that degree was me.

I failed to do so.

I will go to my grave regretting that mistake.

But, the truth is, it was just a mistake—one among many that I have made in my life. Though it cuts me to the quick to think of the damage it did to my father's dreams, the fact is that it happened.

I cannot change it. I cannot take it back. It is a dark part of the legacy that I will leave behind on this earth.

Still, I cannot dwell upon it. The greatest gift I can give myself, and my father, is to forgive that mistake, costly though it may have been in human terms. If I were to dwell upon it, I would lose the joyful moments that remain in my heart about my father, and that single moment would color for all times my memory of the man and our relationship.

Only by forgiving myself can I return the sunlight to my memory of my father. And, perhaps more important, by forgiving myself, I give myself permission to forgive him for his failures and shortcomings in relation to me.

That is the real power of forgiveness. It makes us part of the human family. It acknowledges that we all can do wrong

Kent Nerburn

and that we all need to be embraced and pardoned for acts that we perform and fail to perform.

If we cannot forgive ourselves, we build a wall of defense around our own actions. We twist facts to justify our behaviors, place harsh interpretations on the behaviors of others. Or we sink into an orgy of self-recrimination that keeps us from making any meaningful contribution to life.

But if we can forgive ourselves, we allow ourselves—and those around us—the freedom to be less than perfect. We acknowledge that our shortcomings, and those of others, are but the natural reflections of human beings struggling, by such lights as they have, to do the best they can in this world. We learn to touch the world with a gentler hand.

My friends who cannot forgive their parents are denying themselves that touch. Instead of celebrating the very fact that they were given the gift of life, they are parsing that gift and finding it wanting. They are withholding their forgiveness from those who need it most and, in doing so, are chaining themselves to an interpretation of the world that closes doors on the miracle of possibility.

Whenever I think about forgiveness, I am reminded of the story of Francis and the murderous wolf. According to this tale, a ravenous wolf was terrorizing the countryside around the region of Gubbio, killing all manner of livestock and any humans who happened to be unfortunate enough to be in his path.

Despite the entreaties of the townsfolk, Francis ventured out to talk to the wolf to try to get it to change its ways.

When he finally confronted the beast, he lectured him soundly.

"Brother Wolf," he said, "I am very sorry to hear about the crimes you commit. You have done dreadful deeds, destroying creatures of God without mercy. You deserve an awful death, and I understand why the people of Gubbio hate you. But, Brother Wolf, I want you to make peace with them so they need fear you no more, and you need fear nothing from them or their dogs. If you do so, I will tell the people to feed you as long as you live, for I know that it is hunger that has driven you to act in so horrible a fashion."

The wolf listened intently and, according to the legend, lifted his paw in a pledge to renounce his murderous ways. The townsfolk saw this and rejoiced. From that moment forward, the wolf mended his ways. He lived out his life as a beloved member of the community, going from door to door for food, and was greatly mourned when he died.

The story is probably apocryphal, though, like so many stories of Francis's life, it is so touching that we wish it to be true. But what is important is not its veracity, but the picture it paints of forgiveness, pardon, and reconciliation.

We all carry a wolf within us. It leaps out at unexpected

Kent Nerburn

times and injures those we love, sometimes even murdering their hearts and spirits. We cannot contain it; we cannot bid it be still. If we are human and alive in this world, it will jump out again and again, despite our best efforts to keep it under control, and it will harm others whom we desperately wish that we would not harm.

And the wolves that live in those around us will leap out unexpectedly as well—from our children, from our friends, from our parents, from those we meet in casual conversations. And those wolves will damage us.

What can we do but forgive? Are we so pure as to cast the first stone? Do we alone have the wolf in our hearts under control?

My friends who refuse to forgive their parents are enshrining their anger for all time in their hearts. They are saying that the wolf cannot be forgiven, that its crimes are too great. Do they not realize that their parents, too, were beset by wolves in their own lives, and their parents before them?

Life is too short to freeze our feelings around a moment of wrong, whether it is one that was done to us or one that we have done to others.

If the people of Gubbio had not forgiven the wolf, they would have lived in a state of perpetual anger and rage. Far more than the wolf himself, they would have been prisoners of his crimes.

But they did forgive the wolf, like my friends must forgive their parents, like I must forgive myself, like we all must forgive the world around us for the slights and injuries that have been inflicted upon us and those that we have inflicted on others. And by forgiving him, they once again opened their hearts and set their spirits free.

Each day offers us the opportunity for forgiveness. Someone cuts in front of us in traffic; someone is abrupt to us in conversation; someone we were supposed to meet fails to show up for an appointment; our child or our parent or our spouse hurts us with a harsh word or action. Or maybe we ourselves speak harshly to someone or are unkind to someone in our words or actions.

In all of these instances, the greatest gift we can offer is the gift of forgiveness. Forgiveness is something freely granted, whether earned or deserved; something lovingly offered without thought of acknowledgment or return. It is our way of mirroring the goodness in the heart of a person rather than raising up the harshness of their actions.

But, most of all, it makes us one with the human family and allows us to live in the sunlight of the present, not the darkness of the past. Forgiveness alone, of all our human actions, opens up the world to the miracle of infinite possibility. And that, perhaps, is the closest we can come, in our humble human fashion, to the divine act of bestowing grace.

14

And it is in dying that we are born to eternal life

There are many ways to die. A butterfly dies to the caterpillar when it sheds its chrysalis and takes wing. Francis died to his youthful life of physical pleasures when he stood naked before his father and renounced his worldly goods. A person can die to a previous relationship by committing wholeheartedly to someone new.

Still, most of us, when we think of dying, think only of the death of the body. And so we confront the thought of death with fear and trepidation.

But if we expand our understanding of death to see it as a change of lives, death can be a movement from darkness to light, as surely as from light to darkness. If we look for the deaths that free us to something new and better, we are less inclined to look upon death with fear and more inclined to embrace it with hope.

When Francis tells us that in dying we are born to eternal life, there is no doubt that he is referring to salvation into a life with Christ. And for those of us who can embrace this belief in all its fullness, it offers a balm to the spirit and becomes a polestar around which we can build our entire life and faith.

But even for those of us who are not so certain of the life that awaits us after our physical death, Francis's message still has a great lesson to teach and a great consolation to offer. It reminds us that our actions in this world, and our ability to rise above the limits of our own self-interest, live on far beyond us and play their humble part in shaping a world of spirituality and peace.

Never did this come home to me more clearly than several years ago when I was running a seminar on fatherhood for a group of teachers. On the last evening a Nigerian man was scheduled to come in and drum with us. I had not met him; he had been scheduled independent of my participation. His portion of the programming was insignificant to me, and I looked upon it as little more than a final evening's event that could as easily have been any of a hundred other activities. But the man was scheduled, so I acceded graciously and left the agenda open for him.

On the night of his presentation, he arrived about an hour early with an extensive collection of drums of all colors and shapes and sizes. He conscientiously tuned them and set them out for our use. One by one we shuffled in for his session and took our seats in the circle he had arranged. He had a smile of incredible warmth and a dignity of manner that made us all feel clumsy and rawboned. But his gracious heart quickly took away all our self-consciousness, and soon we were all drumming together and working our way toward a common rhythm and expression.

It was a wonderful experience—far more meaningful than any of us had expected. The man and his drums brought us a joy and camaraderie that had not existed up to the time of his arrival. The music became a metaphor for community, and to a person we were touched by what we had created.

As it neared nine o'clock—the time scheduled for the ending of the event—a number of people asked the man to stay a bit longer.

He smiled graciously but demurred. "I'm sorry," he said, "I have to leave."

Because we had come to feel close to him in our short time together, we pressed him.

"Just a bit longer," we asked.

"I can't," he explained. "I have to catch a plane. I'm going back to Lagos for my mother's funeral."

We were shocked. He had been totally giving to us, totally present, treating us like our activity was the most important event in the world to him. And through it all his heart had been carrying the burden of his mother's death.

"Your mother's funeral?" we asked incredulously.

"Yes," he said. "It was scheduled for last week, and we don't dare put it off again."

"Why was it put off?" someone asked.

"I had said I would come here and be with you," he replied matter-of-factly. "So I had it changed."

"You put off a funeral to be with us?"

The man smiled that deep, warm, loving smile that he had graced us with all evening.

"Oh, yes," he said. "Our funerals aren't like yours. There are many people that have to come."

"How many?" somebody asked.

"About five thousand," he said. "All of her village."

And we, the thirty of us, looked at him. "So you put that off for us?" And he smiled again. "Yes. I had told you I would be here. I am honored that you shared the evening with me, and I thank you."

With that, he left.

We all sat in stunned silence, overwhelmed by the sense of dignity and grace that this man had brought to us. One by one we rose and made our way back to our rooms, lost in our own thoughts and feelings.

There were other activities the following morning—all the presentations, wrap-ups, hugs, and good-byes. But each of our hearts was filled with the indelible image of a gentle man who had changed the time of his mother's funeral a half a world away in order to spend a few hours of time with a group of thirty people he did not know, because he had given us his word.

I do not know that man's name. I cannot even remember what he looked like. In all physical senses, he is as dead to me as if he had passed from this life. And, for all I know, he has. But he has eternal life in my heart as the man who taught me about honor and quiet dignity and graciousness of spirit. And I will try to teach my children what he taught me, and teach my children to teach their children.

In our hearts, this man will never die.

Such events occur in our lives on a daily basis, lodging in our hearts to become part of the legacy of our lives. They form our spirits and touch the spirits of those we touch.

I remember once, as a very young child, seeing an old man and woman crossing the street together. To me they were incalculably old—white haired and bent over, with shaking hands and unsteady limbs.

They moved cautiously toward the curb, then stepped down together. The man took the woman's arm—I can see it today. He held her arm closely as she shuffled into the street, though he himself was unsteady on his feet.

The light changed; the cars began honking. But that man never wavered, never took his eyes or his arm from his wife. He carried her, supported her, though his own legs could hardly stand. And she leaned into him with total faith and confidence, as if he were the very rock of safety itself. Her faith made him stronger. Together they walked through that traffic, buoyed up by each other and their faith in each other's love.

I could not have been more than six. I knew nothing of love's selfless offices. But in that moment I learned more of the steadfastness of love than in all the years since. That man and woman, who never even knew I was watching, set before me a standard to which I will always aspire. With their linked arms and shaking hands, they shaped the clay of my young life.

Like the gentle man from Nigeria, that couple will always be alive for me. When I am tempted to be harsh in my family or find myself wanting to assert my own claims over those of my wife or children, the image of that couple rises up and guides me.

They have eternal life in my heart.

Who is to say what we leave with another when we pass from their life? Though we may no longer be present to them physically, by our words and actions we have shaped some small part of their being. And in passing their life along, they will take what we have shaped in them and use it to help shape another.

All our actions on this earth have eternal life. It is up to us to determine whether our actions have a life that increases the light in the world or adds to the darkness. What Francis calls us to understand is that the actions that increase light in this world are actions that come from the death of self-interest.

The awareness of self is our greatest human conundrum. It is what separates us from others and establishes our individuality, but it is also the one thing we share with all other human beings, so it increases our common humanity.

When we act to serve our self-interest, we increase our separation. When we die to that self-interest, we increase our commonality.

The man who drummed with us had died to his own self-interest, and because of that, he touched us each at a place in the center of our own humanity and will live forever as an instrument of God's peace in all our hearts. The elderly couple, unaware even that they were being observed, were acting in the interests of each other rather than themselves, and in doing so opened the heart of a young boy to the reality of love.

If we can die to the part of us that separates us from others—our individual desires, our self-interests, the attitudes and emotions that build walls around us—and come alive to the part of us that we share in common with others—our human emotions, our capacity for service, our caring for the earth and the things upon it—we can use the self as a way to embrace the world and become one with the hearts of those we meet.

It is a rare and delicate balance, for we can never truly be free of our own sense of self. But we can recognize that it is in divesting ourselves of our own point of view, our own demands, that we truly become open to the world and the magic it contains.

The artist who gives himself over to painting the portrait of another, the nurse who tries to become one with the patient's pain and fear, knows this balance on a daily basis. They walk on a gossamer thread between their own consciousness and that of another, moving back and forth as needed to use their skills to serve the vision to which they are committed.

We all, in our daily lives, are called to walk this same gossamer thread. When we listen to someone with all our heart, not to offer advice but to be present to their fears and dreams; when we give selflessly of our time or energy to help someone in need: these are the times when we are dying to self and coming alive to eternal life. We may not always be able to free ourselves totally from our own self-interest, but if we are fully alive to their interests, that is close enough.

Our lives are our witness, and our witness is our legacy. It is what lives on in the world after we are gone. If our witness is to selfishness, our eternal legacy is one of selfishness. If our witness is to love and kindness and the best of the human heart, it is that which will live on in the hearts of others after we are gone.

Though Francis would have said that by our witness we achieve eternal life in heaven, it is perhaps not so wrong to take a humbler tack and say that what we witness has eternal life here on earth. If what we bind by our actions here on earth is also bound in an eternal realm beyond the veil of knowing, we are all the more blessed.

But it is enough to know that in the great symphony of creation we played our part purely, humbly, and without discordance. When we pass, and our spirit ascends to pierce that one new hole in the midnight sky, we can be sure that the light of God will shine down a bit brighter on this earth. And that somewhere, sometime, one person, coming after us, will stand for a fleeting moment in the presence of that light and know, if only for that moment, that they, too, have been called to be an instrument of God's peace.